WHSmith

Challenge

English

Steve Eddy and
Najoud Ensaff

**Age 11–14
Years 7–9
Key Stage 3**

Acknowledgements

The publishers would like to thank the following for permission to reproduce copyright material:

Soul Eater by Michelle Paver, published by Orion Children's Books. Reprinted by permission of The Orion Publishing Group Ltd.

The Dreamwalker's Child by Steve Voake, Faber Children's Books, 2006.

Troll Fell by Katherine Langrish, Haprer Collins Children's Books, 2005.

'Skivers' by David Williams from *Sport* (editor John Foster), Oxford University Press.

'The Tomcat' by Don Marquis from *The Poolbeg Book of Irish Poetry for Children*, Poolbeg Press, 1997.

My Family and Other Animals by Gerald Durrell, Harper Collins, 2006.

Noughts and Crosses by Malorie Blackman, published by Doubleday. Reprinted by permission of The Random House Group Ltd.

'Holiday Memory' from Collected Stories by Dylan Thomas, published by Orion. Reprinted by permission of David Higham Associates Limited.

'Timothy Winters' from Collected Poems by Charles Causley, published by Picador. Reprinted by permission of David Higham Associates Limited.

Holes by Louis Sacher, Bloosmbury Publishing, 2000.

Animal Farm by George Orwell, A.M. Heath & Co., 1998.

The Most Dangerous Game by Richard Connell, Kessinger Publishers, 2006.

The Moon of Gomrath by Alan Garner, Collins Voyager, 2002.

Point Blanc by Anthony Horowitz, Walker Books, © 2001. Reproduced by permission of Walker Books Ltd, London SE11 5HJ.

'The Hitchhiker' from *The Wonderful Story of Henry Sugar* by Roald Dahl, published by Jonathan Cape Ltd & Penguin Books. Reprinted by permission of David Higham Associates Limited.

The Opposite of Fate by Amy Tan, Harper Perennial, 2004.

Dinosaur article from the BBC Prehistoric section of the BBC website, http://www.bbc.co.uk/sn/prehistoric life/

No More Sitting on the Old School Bench by Alan Bleasdale, Heinemann, 1987.

Antigone by Jean Anouilh, Methuen Drama, 2000.

A View From the Bridge by Arthur Miller, Penguin Modern Classics, 2000.

Empire of the Sun by J.G. Ballard, Harper Perennial Classics, 2006.

War of the Worlds by H.G. Wells, Penguin Classics, 2005. Reproduced by permission of A.P. Watt Ltd. on behalf of the Literary Executors of the Estate of H.G. Wells.

Chessington World of Adventures leaflet: Chessington Operations Limited, a Merlin Entertainments Group Company. A division of Tussauds Theme Parks Limited.

Every effort has been made to reach all copyright holders, but if any have been inadvertently overlooked, the Publishers will be pleased to make the necessary arrangements at the first opportunity.

Although every effort has been made to ensure that website addresses are correct at time of going to press, Hodder Education cannot be held responsible for the content of any website mentioned in this book. It is sometimes possible to find a relocated webpage by typing in the address of the home page for a website in the URL window of your browser.

Hachette UK's policy is to use papers that are natural, renewable and recyclable products and made from wood grown in sustainable forests. The logging and manufacturing processes are expected to conform to the environmental regulations of the country of origin.

Orders: please contact Bookpoint Ltd, 130 Milton Park, Abingdon, Oxon OX14 4SB. Telephone: +44 (0)1235 827720. Fax: +44 (0)1235 400454. Lines are open 9.00a.m.–5.00p.m., Monday to Saturday, with a 24-hour message answering service. Visit our website at www.hoddereducation.co.uk.

© Steve Eddy and Najoud Ensaff 2013
First published in 2007 exclusively for WHSmith by
Hodder Education
An Hachette UK Company
338 Euston Road
London NW1 3BH

Teacher's tips © Najoud Ensaff 2013
This revised edition first published in 2013
Impression number   10 9 8 7 6 5 4 3 2
Year   2018 2017 2016 2015 2014 2013

All rights reserved. Apart from any use permitted under UK copyright law, no part of this publication may be reproduced or transmitted in any form or by any means, electronic or mechanical, including photocopying and recording, or held within any information storage and retrieval system, without permission in writing from the publisher or under licence from the Copyright Licensing Agency Limited. Further details of such licences (for reprographic reproduction) may be obtained from the Copyright Licensing Agency Limited, Saffron House, 6–10 Kirby Street, London EC1N 8TS.

Cover illustration by Oxford Designers and Illustrators Ltd
Illustrations by © Hodder Education
Typeset in Folio Book 10 on 12 pt by DC Graphic Design Ltd, Swanley Village, Kent.
Printed in Spain

A catalogue record for this title is available from the British Library

ISBN 978 1444 189 247

Contents

	Introduction	5
1:	Using evidence	6
2:	Setting and atmosphere	8
3:	A cast of characters	10
4:	Mood	12
5:	What do *you* think of it?	14
6:	Form and meaning in poetry	16
7:	Playscripts	18
8:	Good intentions – a writer's purpose	20
9:	The writer's intentions – audience	22
10:	Tugging on heartstrings: emotive writing	24
11:	A day in the life of …	26
12:	Poetry experiment	28
13:	Character building	30
14:	Creative conflict	32
15:	Descriptive delight	34
16:	Roving reporter	36
17:	Insider report	38
18:	Independent research	40
19:	Themes	42
20:	Fact, opinion and bias	44
21:	Irony and satire	46
22:	Structure: the shape of a text	48
23:	Comparing texts	50
24:	What is context	52
25:	Genre	54
26:	Form in poetry	56
27:	Planning a character analysis	58
28:	Party parody	60

29: 'The Dream Woman'	62
30: Quality not quantity	64
31: All about me	66
32: How? What? Why?	68
33: A balancing act	70
34: Synthesising information	72
35: Comparing texts – ideas	74
36: Comparing texts – values	76
37: Comparing texts – emotions	78
38: Comparing modern and older texts	80
39: Dramatic impact	82
40: Shakespeare's world – the context	84
41: Shakespeare's language	86
42: Tragedy, comedy, history	88
43: Plot and themes: comedy	90
44: Characterisation in a tragedy	92
45: Values in a history play	94
46: Planning an essay on a theme	96
47: Writing an essay on a theme	98
48: Writing a playscript	100
49: Writing to create a mood	102
50: Writing in role	104
51: Narrative voice	106
52: A science fiction experiment	108
53: Writing a sonnet	110
54: Persuasive politics	112
55: An enticing leaflet	114
Answers	116

Introduction

English Challenge KS3 has been written by two educational writers and examiners who have, between them, over 30 years' teaching experience.

This book aims to stimulate lower secondary school age children. It includes a range of activities to develop reading and writing skills beyond what would normally be experienced in school lessons.

English Challenge KS3 extends students so that they can experience and enjoy English at a higher level.

Readers are presented with reading and writing tasks that are loosely based on the National Literacy Framework but which seek to enrich students' understanding and experience of English. Each double-page section deals with a separate topic.

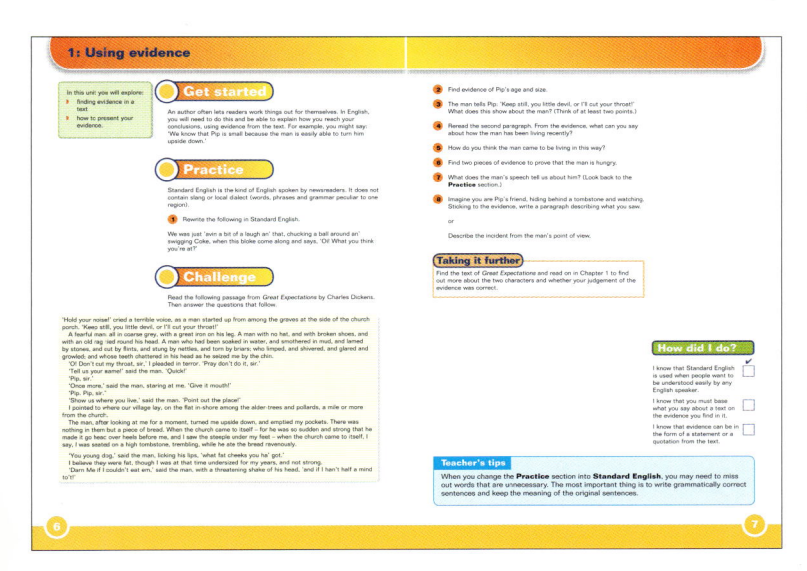

Each unit is divided into digestible subsections of: **Get started**, **Practice**, **Challenge** and **How did I do?**

An introductory box outlines what the focus of the unit will be and the **Get started** section provides more detail about the topic.

The **Practice** section allows students to consider the topic at word or sentence level before the **Challenge** section, which provides students with challenging and interesting extracts that they might not normally encounter in school. The activities aim to stimulate students' imagination and extend their understanding and skills. Where appropriate they are given hints on tasks.

The **Taking it further** boxes suggest extra sources for further research or more demanding tasks. In **How did I do?**, students are encouraged to consider what they have learnt and the skills that they have developed.

The **Teacher's Tips** help deepen the students' understanding and confidence. The **Answers** section gives guidance on possible responses. Fuller answers are provided for the Reading sections but the Writing sections only have answers where these have been practical.

1: Using evidence

In this unit you will explore:
- finding evidence in a text
- how to present your evidence.

Get started

An author often lets readers work things out for themselves. In English, you will need to do this and be able to explain how you reach your conclusions, using evidence from the text. For example, you might say: 'We know that Pip is small because the man is easily able to turn him upside down.'

Practice

Standard English is the kind of English spoken by newsreaders. It does not contain slang or local dialect (words, phrases and grammar peculiar to one region).

1 Rewrite the following in Standard English.

We was just 'avin a bit of a laugh an' that, chucking a ball around an' swigging Coke, when this bloke come along and says, 'Oi! What you think you're at?'

Challenge

Read the following passage from *Great Expectations* by Charles Dickens. Then answer the questions that follow.

'Hold your noise!' cried a terrible voice, as a man started up from among the graves at the side of the church porch. 'Keep still, you little devil, or I'll cut your throat!'

A fearful man, all in coarse grey, with a great iron on his leg. A man with no hat, and with broken shoes, and with an old rag tied round his head. A man who had been soaked in water, and smothered in mud, and lamed by stones, and cut by flints, and stung by nettles, and torn by briars; who limped, and shivered, and glared and growled; and whose teeth chattered in his head as he seized me by the chin.

'O! Don't cut my throat, sir,' I pleaded in terror. 'Pray don't do it, sir.'

'Tell us your name!' said the man. 'Quick!'

'Pip, sir.'

'Once more,' said the man, staring at me. 'Give it mouth!'

'Pip. Pip, sir.'

'Show us where you live,' said the man. 'Point out the place!'

I pointed to where our village lay, on the flat in-shore among the alder-trees and pollards, a mile or more from the church.

The man, after looking at me for a moment, turned me upside down, and emptied my pockets. There was nothing in them but a piece of bread. When the church came to itself – for he was so sudden and strong that he made it go head over heels before me, and I saw the steeple under my feet – when the church came to itself, I say, I was seated on a high tombstone, trembling, while he ate the bread ravenously.

'You young dog,' said the man, licking his lips, 'what fat cheeks you ha' got.'

I believe they were fat, though I was at that time undersized for my years, and not strong.

'Darn Me if I couldn't eat em,' said the man, with a threatening shake of his head, 'and if I han't half a mind to't!'

2 Find evidence of Pip's age and size.

3 The man tells Pip: 'Keep still, you little devil, or I'll cut your throat!' What does this show about the man? (Think of at least two points.)

4 Reread the second paragraph. From the evidence, what can you say about how the man has been living recently?

5 How do you think the man came to be living in this way?

6 Find two pieces of evidence to prove that the man is hungry.

7 What does the man's speech tell us about him? (Look back to the **Practice** section.)

8 Imagine you are Pip's friend, hiding behind a tombstone and watching. Sticking to the evidence, write a paragraph describing what you saw.

or

Describe the incident from the man's point of view.

Taking it further

Find the text of *Great Expectations* and read on in Chapter 1 to find out more about the two characters and whether your judgement of the evidence was correct.

How did I do?

- I know that Standard English is used when people want to be understood easily by any English speaker. ☐
- I know that you must base what you say about a text on the evidence you find in it. ☐
- I know that evidence can be in the form of a statement or a quotation from the text. ☐

Teacher's tips

When you change the **Practice** section into **Standard English**, you may need to miss out words that are unnecessary. The most important thing is to write grammatically correct sentences and keep the meaning of the original sentences.

2: Setting and atmosphere

In this unit you will explore:
- setting – the time and place in which the action of a story occurs
- atmosphere – the feeling created by the use of setting
- how atmosphere prepares us for events.

Get started

An author must give readers some idea of the different settings in which the events of a story occur. There are two reasons for this.

- It makes it easier to picture what happens.
- A setting prepares us for what happens by creating the right atmosphere.

Practice

1. Here are some adjectives that might be used to describe settings.

sunlit	crumbling	towering	dazzling
fashionable	bustling	bleak	lush

   Look them up in a dictionary if necessary. Then make up sentences using them to describe settings.

   Example: *The **lush** foliage was alive with pink hummingbirds.*

2. Match up the adjectives with settings from the following list. (Note: there is more than one possible match for each setting.)

   - a meadow with grazing cows
   - the seaside
   - a ruined castle
   - a street
   - a garden
   - moorland on a grey winter's day
   - a celebrity's front room
   - a mountain pass

Challenge

In *Soul Eater* by Michelle Paver, a Stone Age boy called Torak and his friend, a girl called Renn, are trying to rescue Wolf (a wolf!) from a group of evil 'Soul Eaters'. The pair have tracked the Soul Eaters to a cave entrance.

> Above them reared the gaunt mountain, lit crimson by the last rays of the sun. In its flank, a black hole gaped. Before it, like a warning, stood a tall grey pillar of stone.
>
> White mist seeped from the darkness of the cave. Clammy tendrils reached for them, stinking of dread and demons. Hope fled. If the Soul Eaters had taken Wolf in there . . . .
>
> Glancing over her shoulder, Renn saw the shape of the whole mountain for the first time. She saw how it rose out of the snow like the head of some giant creature. She saw how the ice river uncoiled its sinuous bulk east, before twisting round to lose itself in the Sea.

> Torak had seen it too. 'We've found the Viper,' he whispered.
> 'We're standing on it,' breathed Renn.
> They turned back to the mountain: to the glaring black hole split by the standing stone.
> 'And there's the Eye,' she said.

The language of the passage builds up an atmosphere that fits in with what is happening – and what is about to happen. Answer the following questions.

3 How does the time of day affect the atmosphere?

4 Why could the word 'crimson' make us think of danger?

5 How does the author make the mountain sound threatening? (Hint: look for two sentences and think of her choice of words.)

6 How does the way the cave entrance (the 'black hole') is described make it seem threatening?

7 How does the way the mist is described affect the atmosphere?

8 What effect does the name given to the ice river have?

9 What kind of action do you think will occur next?

10 What atmosphere is created in the following passage and what kind of events would you expect to follow?

> The disused factory stood by the rusting railway line. It had been derelict for years. The cracked concrete surrounding it was strewn with litter and broken glass. One huge metal door stood slightly open, like a trap. I drew in my breath and squeezed through the gap into a twilight world of looming shadows, silent machinery and dust.

Taking it further

Find the text of *Bleak House* by Charles Dickens (try www.online-literature.com/view.php/bleakhouse). Read the first paragraph in Chapter 1, beginning 'Fog everywhere'. Decide what atmosphere is created.

How did I do?

I know that setting includes place, time of day and weather.

I know that the language used to describe the setting is a major factor in creating atmosphere.

I know that the atmosphere prepares us for the action.

Teacher's tips

Reading a passage aloud or listening to a passage being read aloud while you keep your eyes closed will help you to imagine the setting and sense the atmosphere.

3: A cast of characters

In this unit you will explore:
- how authors portray characters in fiction
- the importance of viewpoint.

Get started

These are the most important ways in which authors reveal characters:

- what they do
- what they say
- what they think
- physical appearance
- what other characters say about them
- direct description ('Thea was a shy girl . . .').

Practice

Adjectives (such as 'shy') can describe a character, but verbs also tell us a great deal.

1 In the following sentences, what do the verbs tell us about the characters?

   a Jack strode across the room, a wide smile on his face.
   b She strutted down the corridor, ignoring me completely.
   c 'How dare you!' she spat, her eyes blazing.
   d He sprawled across the grass, his eyes studying the passers-by.
   e 'But w-why me?' she faltered.

Challenge

In *The Dreamwalker's Child* by Steve Voake, a boy, Sam, finds himself in another world where the sinister General Hekken wants information from him.

Hekken smiled again, but his eyes were cold; dead as a fish on a slab.
   The punch, when it came, was so hard that it sent Sam sprawling against the wall and left him clutching his stomach in agony. Hekken grabbed him by the front of his prison uniform and pulled him to his feet again.
   'Don't lie to me,' he hissed, his voice full of venom. 'I own you, do you hear me? You belong to me now. Understand?'
   He threw Sam back into the corner with such force that all the wind was knocked out of him and he collapsed in a heap on the wet floor.
   'I'll give you a few hours to think about it,' he said, turning back to look at Sam from the doorway. 'If you can't come up with something better, then I'm afraid I will have to arrange another meeting with your friends from the train.' He shook his head sadly. 'They mean well, of course, but between you and me . . .' Here he paused, then whispered in a conspiratorial voice, 'They can be awfully unpleasant. Just something for you to think about, that's all. I look forward to discussing it with you later.'
   The door slammed shut.

2 Think about how Hekken smiles. Try smiling at yourself in a mirror – but only with your mouth, not your eyes. What is the effect?

3 What do Hekken's cold, dead eyes suggest about him?

4 What characteristic does the second paragraph reveal about Hekken?

5 What exactly is suggested by the phrase 'he hissed, his voice full of venom'?

6 After Hekken's outburst, his approach changes. What is the effect of the phrase 'I'm afraid I will have to arrange another meeting with your friends from the train'? (The 'friends' are some human-headed police dogs that attacked Sam on the train!)
(Hint: is Hekken really reluctant to 'arrange' this meeting?)

7 Why does Steve Voake describe Hekken as speaking in a 'conspiratorial' voice? Look up the word if necessary.

8 Would you describe Hekken as a straightforward man? If not, why not?

Viewpoint refers to the point of view from which an author tells a story. It can be third person (he, she, him, her . . .), as in the extract above, or first person (I, me).

9 Summarise what happens in the passage above, telling the story from Sam's viewpoint, to reveal what you think Sam might be like. (He's the hero of the novel.)

10 Now sum up the passage telling the story from Hekken's viewpoint. (Hint: how might Hekken describe Sam? How might he describe his own methods?)

A clever way to reveal a character is to tell the story in the third person but to hint at the characters' thoughts and feelings.

Example: 'Hekken looked at the boy. He was not going to let this miserable little worm get the better of him . . .'

11 Continue the description in this style.

How did I do?

☑ I know that authors reveal characters by what they do, say and think, their looks, what others say about them, and by direct description. ☐

I know that authors can write in the third or first person and that either of these can reveal character. ☐

Teacher's tips

For question 9 and question 10, remember to refer to your thoughts and feelings. If you were Sam how would you feel? If you were Hekken what would you think?

4: Mood

In this unit you will explore:
- what 'mood' means in fiction
- what techniques writers use to create mood.

Get started

Mood is the feeling that authors create by what happens in a story and what words they choose to describe it.

Practice

Authors have to choose adjectives carefully to create mood. Often, two or more adjectives can have similar meanings but create a slightly different mood.

1 Choose the most appropriate adjective in the sentences below.

   a Her voice was (soft/squashy/flabby).
   b The (skinny/wizened/thin) old wizard's eyes contained the wisdom of centuries.
   c In one (speedy/hasty/swift) movement she was at my side.
   d 'It is an (ancient/elderly/old-fashioned) custom of our people,' she said respectfully.

Challenge

In *Troll Fell* by Katherine Langrish, a Viking boy, Peer, meets a witch-like water spirit, Granny Greenteeth. She tries to lure him to his death in the deep water of a millpond.

> She stretched out her arms to him and her voice became a low musical murmur like the stream in summer. 'I'll take you – I'll love you – I'll look after you. Who else will? I'll give you an everlasting bed. Come with me, down under the water and rest. Rest your weary bones.'
>
>   The rank, rotten, water smells grew stronger and stronger. White mist rose from the surface of the millpond, flowing in soft wreaths over the plank bridge and swirling gently around his knees. His teeth chattered and his head swam. He could no longer see the bridge or the water. How easy it would be to let go, to fall into the soft mist. All for the best, maybe.
>
>   'All for the bessst,' Granny Greenteeth agreed in a soft hiss.
>
>   Far away a dog barked. Loki? Peer blinked, suddenly wide awake. He looked at the old woman. 'No!' he said slowly. 'Loki needs me. No! I won't!'
>
>   There was a whisper of wind. The mist blew away into the willows.

2 Read Granny Greenteeth's words aloud. What is their effect, and what phrase describes their sound?

3 *Alliteration* is the repetition of consonant sounds (for example, 'big bang') for effect. Find examples of it here (you should be able to find four). How do they affect the mood?

4 What is the effect of the mist on the mood – and of it blowing away at the end?

5 What sound changes the mood near the end of the passage, and how does it do this?

6 What phrase tells us that Peer is almost persuaded by Granny Greenteeth?

7 Find at least three phrases that appeal to our senses in order to create mood.

8 Describe the mood of this passage up to the point when it changes.

One of the things that affects mood is rhythm. In the *Troll Fell* passage, the author makes Granny Greenteeth speak in a rhythmic way to hypnotise Peer.

In the passage below, from Shakespeare's *Macbeth*, Macbeth has just murdered the King.

> **Macbeth**: I have done the deed. Didst thou not hear a noise?
>
> **Lady Macbeth**: I heard the owl scream and the crickets cry. Did not you speak?
>
> **Macbeth**: When?
>
> **Lady Macbeth**: Now.
>
> **Macbeth**: As I descended?
>
> **Lady Macbeth**: Ay.
>
> **Macbeth**: Hark! Who lies i' the second chamber?
>
> **Lady Macbeth**: Donalbain.
>
> **Macbeth**: This is a sorry sight. [*Looking on his hands*]

9 How do the short sentences affect the mood?

Taking it further

List as many possible moods for writing as you can. Use plain paper and write your words in an appropriate visual style. For example, use big bubbly letters for 'Happy' and jagged letters for 'Angry'.

How did I do?

	✔
I know that mood is the feeling that an author creates in fiction.	☐
I know that authors choose words carefully to create mood.	☐
I know that the rhythm of sentences has an effect on mood.	☐

Teacher's tips

For question 3 think about whether the repeated **consonant sounds** are soft or hard. This will help you to determine the effects of the **alliteration**.

5: What do *you* think of it?

> In this unit you will explore:
> - why your own views on a text are important
> - how to interpret and evaluate a text.

Get started

In English, you will often be asked to *interpret* and *evaluate* a text.

To *interpret* it is to say what it means to you, backing your ideas up with evidence from the text.

To *evaluate* it is to say how effective you think it is, and why.

Practice

Authors make choices, for example about *similes*.

1 In each sentence below, decide which simile is the most appropriate, and why.

  a The enemy's arrows fell upon us like (daggers / a deadly rain / express trains).
  b The river twisted through the valley like (a diamond / a giant snake / a silver ribbon).
  c With the snarling dogs close behind, I forced myself into the escape tunnel. I felt like (a rat in a drainpipe / a bullet in a gun barrel / a stick of rock in its wrapper).

Challenge

Read the following passage and consider:

- possible interpretations of the characters' behaviour
- how effective the writing is.

The picnic was going well. My cousin Justin was full of surprises. Now he was entertaining us with a battered harmonica. In between numbers, we listened to ecstatic skylarks and the river slip-sliding past.

'Know anything from the 80s, Justin?' asked Dad, hopefully.

'Justin's 14, dear,' said Mum with practised patience.

I pulled a face. 'Hey – is there another ham sandwich?'

'Finish that one,' said Mum.

It was then that things started to go wrong. First, a gun went off like a cannon a few fields away. Our boxer dog Boris started to bark madly.

'Stop that, Boris!' Dad yelled at him. 'It's just the farmer shooting rooks,' he added to us. Boris whimpered pathetically.

'Poor Boris!' I said, patting him with exaggerated sympathy. To cheer him up I threw a stick, but my aim was poor, and it splashed into the river. Undeterred, Boris shot off like a train, straight through our picnic. Overturning a bowl of pink Angel Delight, he plunged excitedly into the river.

'Oh no – the pudding!' wailed Mum.

'He'll soak us when he comes out!' said Dad.

But I noticed that Justin was on his feet and pointing in the opposite direction. 'Look,' he said in a low, hoarse voice. 'That cow – it's a bull!'

2 How do *you* interpret the following lines? In other words, what meaning do you think lies behind them?

  a 'said Mum with practised patience'
  b 'I pulled a face'
  c 'he said in a low, hoarse voice'

3 Why do you think the skylarks are described as 'ecstatic'?

4 How effective do you find the following words and phrases, and why?

  a 'the river slip-sliding past'
  b 'a gun went off like a cannon'
  c 'Boris shot off like a train'

5 How effectively do you think the author:

  a interests us in the characters
  b creates a lively scene
  c creates suspense about what will happen next?

6 Write your own replacements for the phrases given in questions 2, 3 and 4. Make them as effective as you can.

7 Write a paragraph giving your overall assessment of this passage and explaining why you would, or would not, want to read on.

8 Read the following alternative version of the opening to the passage opposite. Spot the differences and compare their effectiveness.

> Our picnic was going like a dream. My cousin Justin was an intriguing character. Now he was playing a harmonica that looked as if it had been run over by a bus. Between numbers, we listened to cheerful skylarks and the river running past.
>   'Know any songs from the 80s, Justin?' asked Dad, hopefully.
>   'Don't be silly, darling, Justin's only 14,' sighed Mum.
>   I grimaced. 'Hey – is there another ham sandwich?'
>   'Finish that one,' snapped Mum.
>   It was then that things started to go wrong. First, a gun exploded a few fields away. Our dog Boris started to bark like a thing possessed.

How did I do?

- I know that authors make word choices. ☐
- I know that it is up to the reader to interpret a text. ☐
- I know that I should learn to evaluate the effectiveness of texts. ☐

Teacher's tips

Remember, when you use a comparison in a **simile**, the compared object needs to make sense and suggest something particular about the original object – what it looks like, feels like, sounds like etc.

The sun rose in the sky like a car would not be a good **simile** but *The sun rose in the sky like an angel* would.

6: Form and meaning in poetry

In this unit you will explore:
- how the meanings of words change over time
- how the form of a poem *helps* to shape its meaning
- what techniques poets use.

Get started

One difference between poetry and prose is that in poetry the line-lengths are an important part of the form, whereas prose simply runs on from one line to the next. This is just one of the ways in which *form* is important in poetry. Others are rhythm, rhyme and alliteration.

Practice

Words change their meanings over the years. This is because people use them in different ways. Other words fall out of use.

1. Read the following phrases from 'Elegy Written in a Country Churchyard', written in 1751 by Thomas Gray, and suggest what they mean. Concentrate especially on the *italicised* words.

   a. 'o'er the *lea*'
   b. '*Save* where the beetle wheels his *droning* flight'
   c. '*yonder* ivy-*mantled* tower'
   d. '*Molest* her ancient solitary reign'
   e. 'The *rude* forefathers of the hamlet sleep'

Challenge

Now read the extract from Gray's poem below (aloud if you can) and answer the questions that follow.

> The curfew tolls the knell of parting day,
> The lowing herd wind slowly o'er the lea
> The plowman homeward plods his weary way,
> And leaves the world to darkness and to me.
>
> Now fades the glimmering landscape on the sight,
> And all the air a solemn stillness holds,
> Save where the beetle wheels his droning flight,
> And drowsy tinklings lull the distant folds;
>
> Save that from yonder ivy-mantled tower
> The moping owl does to the moon complain
> Of such, as wand'ring near her secret bower,
> Molest her ancient solitary reign.
>
> Beneath those rugged elms, that yew-tree's shade,
> Where heaves the turf in many a mould'ring heap,
> Each in his narrow cell for ever laid,
> The rude forefathers of the hamlet sleep.

2 How does the time of day (late afternoon or early evening) affect the poet's mood?

3 What is meant by the first line? (Look up any words you do not understand.)

4 Express in your own words what three things in verse 1 mark the end of the day.

5 What two things in verse 2 break the 'solemn stillness' (the silence)?

6 In verse 3, what do you think the owl is complaining about to the moon? (A 'bower' is a leafy hiding place.)

7 In the last verse, what do you think makes the churchyard turf (grass) heave up 'in many a mould'ring heap'?

8 This poem is written in very even verses, in a steady rhythm. There are the same number of syllables in every line, and they are all in *iams* (they sound like di-<u>dum</u>, di-<u>dum</u> . . .). How does this regular form add to the meaning of the poem?

9 The *rhyme scheme* (the sequence in which lines rhyme) is also very regular. Which words rhyme in verse 1, for example?

Gray adds to the effect of the rhythm and rhyme by using *alliteration* – repeated sounds at the beginning of words – in phrases such as 'weary way' and 'solemn stillness'. So we have repetition in the rhythm and the sound of the words.

10 How do you think this adds to the meaning and the mood? (Hint: the poet is not writing about an unusual event, or about things changing.)

11 Find Gray's Elegy (available online) and read it. Write about the overall effect of the poem and how its form affects its meaning.

12 Find a play by Shakespeare and compare the rhythm of Shakespeare's verse with that of Gray's poem. (Hint: speak the lines aloud and tap out the rhythm, counting the syllables.)

13 Find a poem called 'The Windhover' by Gerard Manley Hopkins (available online). This begins 'I caught this morning morning's minion . . .'. How does it differ in form, mood and meaning from Gray's poem?

How did I do?

	✓
I know that words change their meaning over time.	☐
I know that in poetry, rhythm, rhyme and word sounds (especially alliteration) add to the meaning.	☐

Teacher's tips

If you have difficulty with question 1, you can use the **Oxford English Dictionary online** which provides the origins of words and also defines some older words.

7: Playscripts

In this unit you will explore:
- how playscripts are different from other texts
- what dramatic tension is
- how a play reveals its characters.

Get started

Plays tell their stories and reveal their characters in ways that make them different from novels. A play cannot have description ('It was a beautiful day in spring . . .') or comment on characters ('She was a strange girl . . .'). It has to depend on what the characters say and do.

Practice

All drama involves tension. Usually this is when two or more characters want different things, but sometimes the tension is within one character who is pulled in conflicting directions. What holds our interest is our desire to find out how the tension is resolved.

1 What possible tension could there be in the following situations?

   a A father and son go fishing.
   b A mother wants her son to do well at school and go to university.
   c Two boys make friends with a girl who lives on their street.
   d A girl is a promising gymnast but likes being popular.
   e A boy really wants to buy his mother a present but has no money.

Challenge

This extract is from a play by David Williams called *Skivers*. Two schoolgirls have to take part in a race at school. Read the first part and answer the questions that follow.

> MISS DUNN: Right girls. Everybody line up behind the flags, please. *[Crowded commotion]* Don't push. Spread yourselves right down the track.
> HELEN: Not fair, miss. The ones at the front get a start on us.
> MISS DUNN: It's four miles, Helen. I'm sure you'll catch up.
> CLAIRE: *[Mimicking]* Not fair, miss.
> PAULA: I don't see why everybody has to run. Why don't they just let the Helen Clarks an' them get on with it. They'll win anyway. We could just stay and cheer.
> CLAIRE: Wouldn't cheer that stuck-up thing.

2 What tension or conflict is there at this point?

3 As a reader or audience member, what question do you want to have answered at this point?

> MISS DUNN: Claire Morton! What are you doing with your coat on?
> CLAIRE: It's freezing, miss.
> MISS DUNN: Don't be stupid. You can't run in that.
> CLAIRE: Don't want to run.
> MISS DUNN: Take it off.
> CLAIRE: Nowhere to put it.
> MISS DUNN: Give it here. Get into line. You too, Paula Wood. *[Calling]* Everybody ready?

4 What new tension is there? What do you think will happen next?

> [*Gun fires. A stampede*]
> CLAIRE: [*Running*] Hang on, Paula. Don't run so rotten fast.
> PAULA: I'm getting carried away with the rest.
> CLAIRE: We'll be carried off if we keep this pace up. Four miles and we're not out the gate yet.
> PAULA: Helen Clark is.
> CLAIRE: Slow down.
> PAULA: We're last now.
> CLAIRE: Good. That way nobody'll see us skiving off.
> PAULA: How d'you mean?
> CLAIRE: My house is just round the corner. Let's nip in there for a cup of coffee.
> PAULA: We can't do that. We'll be miles behind.
> CLAIRE: They come back the same way, stupid. We'll just tuck in behind them. Nobody'll know.
> PAULA: I don't . . .
> CLAIRE: What's the problem?
> PAULA: I don't want people calling me a cheat . . .
> CLAIRE: They won't know. Anyway, it's not as if we're trying to win. We're going to be last in any case, so what's the diff . . . Come on, if you're that keen on running I'll race you to my house.

5 Which girl first suggests getting out of the race? What does this tell us about her character?

6 How does the other girl respond to the suggestion and what does this tell us about her?

7 The play continues. What questions do you want answered about what might happen? How does this hold the audience's interest?

8 Rewrite the extract as a story. Include the things that you cannot have in a script; for example, description of the girls and what goes on in their minds.

9 Continue the story as prose fiction or in the form of a playscript.

10 Write a set of director's notes telling the actors who play the girls how to perform their parts in a stage play.

11 How would you present the script for television? What shots would you emphasise?

How did I do?

	✓
I know that plays tell their story through action and speech.	☐
I know that plays depend on dramatic tension to hold our interest.	☐
I know that characters are revealed through what they say and do.	☐

Teacher's tips

For question 11, some key words that may come in handy are: *pan, close-up, zoom, long shot*. Why don't you do an internet search to get some ideas about how the script could be filmed?

8: Good intentions – a writer's purpose

In this unit you will explore:
- what is meant by a writer's *intention* or *purpose*
- what possible purposes there are in non-fiction
- how writers match style to purpose.

Get started

Any piece of writing has a purpose – also called the writer's *intention*. This is the effect the author wants to have on the reader. Good writers match style to purpose.

Practice

1. Think of as many purposes in writing as you can. For example, one major purpose is to *entertain*.

Challenge

2. Read the following passages. For each passage, identify a purpose, and explain how you can tell that this is the purpose.

   The following questions should help you.

   - What adjectives are used?
   - Is the language factual or imaginative?
   - Are there any opinions?
   - Is any advice given?

a I regretted my choice of Hallowe'en costume almost as soon as I arrived. The guests included several young witches, in black velvet, fishnet tights and purple eye make-up. Two or three Draculas eyed me pityingly while fingering their fangs. Their costumes were sophisticated and flattering. Mine was less so: I was a gorilla.

b Puddletown Operatic Society's production of *The Hobbit* was a partial success. Gandalf (Derek Mobley) was convincingly wise and twinkly-eyed, while our hairy-footed little hero (Ian Hobbs) sang bravely, if not always in tune. However, it was surely a mistake to make Gollum (Ethel Plunkett) a singing part . . .

c There are certain rules cyclists should follow to avoid disaster. Make sure your bike is in good repair – especially the brakes; always wear a helmet; and never assume that car drivers have seen you.

d Snowdonia's highest peak is Snowdon itself. This can be climbed by a number of routes, some more challenging than others. On the other hand, there is also a train which travels up the north side from Llanberis, to reach a café on top. This is shut in winter.

e Mallorca is an underrated holiday destination. Its capital, Palma, has fashionable shops, historic churches, and an ancient Arab bath-house. Outside the city, there are pretty hilltop villages, and rugged scenery ideal for walkers. The island is also a great spot for bird-watchers and cyclists.

3 Here is another extract written with a clear purpose. Decide what that purpose is and how it differs from the purpose of Extract **e** in question 2.

> School uniform does little for pupil equality, as some pupils look better in it than others, and some have to wear cast-offs from older brothers and sisters. Moreover, clothes are a means of self-expression, and school uniform crushes individuality.

4 Write a paragraph of your own with the same purpose, on the same subject.

Jonathan Swift was a satirical writer – one who used grim humour to criticise society. In 1729 he wrote 'A Modest Proposal' suggesting what should be done with poor children in Ireland.

5 Read this extract and suggest Swift's purpose and why he writes in such a calm, matter-of-fact way.

> I have been assured by a very knowing American of my acquaintance in London, that . . . a young healthy child well nursed is at a year old a most delicious, nourishing, and wholesome food, whether stewed, roasted, baked, or boiled; and I make no doubt that it will equally serve in a fricassée or a ragout.
>
> I do therefore humbly offer it to public consideration that [the majority of poor Irish children] at a year old, be offered in the sale to the persons of quality and fortune through the kingdom; always advising the mother to let them suck plentifully in the last month, so as to render them plump and fat for a good table.

Taking it further

Try to find examples of the following purposes in books, magazines and newspapers:

- to entertain
- to advise
- to persuade
- to complain.

How effective do you think each one is, and why?

How did I do?

- I know that a writer's intention or purpose is the effect he or she wants to have on readers.
- I know that all writing has at least one of several possible purposes.
- I know that good writers make their style match their purpose.

Teacher's tips

When you read the extract written by Swift, think about whether the writer meant what he wrote or whether he was trying to create a certain effect. For example, if I look outside and see torrential rain for the third day in a row, and I say, 'It's sunny again!' what effect do you think I am trying to create?

9: The writer's intentions – audience

In this unit you will explore:
- what is meant by a writer's *audience*
- some possible audiences
- how writers match their style to their intended audience.

Get started

Most writing has an intended *audience* in mind. The audience means the readership at whom a piece of writing is targeted. It could be:

- young or old
- educated or less educated
- male, female or both
- interested in a specialist area, or not
- reading while in a particular place, for example on a plane.

Practice

1. Write audience *profiles* (short descriptions) for the following book titles.

- Teddy's Special Day
- First Steps In Tropical Fish Care
- The Great Philosophers: the roots of knowledge
- Coping with Parents
- Europe on a Dollar a Day
- Up Everest the Hard Way

Challenge

2. Read the following passages. For each passage, identify a likely audience, and explain how you came to this decision.

The following questions should help you.

- What level of language is used?
- Does the writing assume specialist interest or knowledge?
- How does the author address the reader?
- Is the language formal (serious and correct) or informal (relaxed and casual)?

a You will spend three days in the beautiful Wye Valley, where J.K. Rowling spent her childhood years. There will be an opportunity to visit her secondary school and to shop in the quaint old border town of Chepstow, an inspiration to Ms Rowling's novels, and to meet one of her old English teachers . . .

b Let's face it, gals, brothers are a trial. Just when you're listening to your fave download, your darling bro thinks it's cool to pull your plug. But they do have their uses. They can explain the offside rule to you, and, er . . . that's it!

c Mrs Wallaby was hopping to the shops one day when she heard a loud bang. 'What was that?' she said to herself. Just then, round the corner came Mr Wallaby – driving a big red car!

d Use the three tyre levers to prise off the tyre, hooking each one round a spoke at roughly six-inch intervals. Work the levers round until you have removed the tyre . . .

3 Here is a more challenging magazine extract. Who are the target audience? Explain what phrases lead you to your conclusions.

Breaking news! Five long years of digging at Sparrow Swallet have finally paid off. Members of Bleasdale CC are celebrating a major breakthrough, led by Andy Jarvis, Freddy 'the Ferret' Fernley, and Kate Jenkins. On a routine digging trip, the intrepid trio removed a large boulder to reveal a body-sized phreatic tube leading to a large and well-decorated chamber. A stream passage continues for 300 metres before finally becoming too tight to follow. Surveying is in process.

4 Shakespeare wrote his plays for everyone – educated and uneducated. In this extract from his play *Macbeth*, spot the words that would appeal to his educated audience and those that would be understood by the less educated.

Will all great Neptune's ocean wash this blood
Clean from my hand? No, this my hand will rather
The multitudinous seas incarnadine,
Making the green one red.

5 Suggest audiences for the following magazines, based on what you find in their websites.

- *Sidewalk* magazine (www.sidewalkmag.com)
- *Moderndog* magazine (www.moderndogmagazine.com)
- *New Scientist* (www.newscientist.com)

How did I do?

- I know that a writer's audience is the group of people at which the writing is aimed. ✓
- I know audiences vary in many ways, including age, gender, education, and specialist interest and knowledge.
- I know that good writers make their style match their audience.

Teacher's tips

When you respond to question 3, it may help you to read over the extract a few times. Look out for key and repeated words which may give you a clue about what the extract is about and who the audience might be.

10: Tugging on heartstrings: emotive writing

In this unit you will explore:
- what is meant by *emotive* writing
- what emotions writers play on
- how language plays on our emotions.

Get started

Emotive writing is persuasive writing that goes beyond simply presenting reasoned arguments. Its language is deliberately biased and aims to change the way the reader feels about a subject.

Practice

1. Pair the emotive words and phrases below with the subjects and add to them to create persuasive sentences. (Use a dictionary if necessary.)

   Example: *brutal* and *foxes* – Foxes are the innocent victims of brutal huntsmen.

Words/phrases	Subjects
brutal	famine victims
plundered	puppies
emaciated	poverty
abandoned	foxes
lap of luxury	Mother Earth

Challenge

2. Read the following passages. For each one, copy out at least one emotive word or phrase. Then describe the emotion that it appeals to and how it makes its effect on readers. To get you started, the emotive words and phrases in the first passage are in *italic*.

a When the soldiers rode away on their *well-fed* horses, they left our *women and children butchered in the snow*. We survivors were *herded* into the reservation – all that was left of our land. The white men's promises were *like twigs* – easily broken.

b As you tuck into your turkey, spare a thought for Meg, shivering in a shop doorway and scavenging scraps from bins. Her future is bleak, but your gift could make a difference. There again, if you don't care enough, don't let us spoil your Christmas.

c The planet groans beneath the weight of our indifference. Our factories poison our air, our gas-guzzling cars pump out deadly carbons that heat up our earth like a fried egg. The rainforest – our greatest natural resource – is being ripped out so that we can eat more hamburgers.

d We are being held hostage by young hoodlums who prowl the streets looking for their next victim. Their shoplifting ruins local businesses and they terrorise the elderly – who deserve peace and quiet – in their own homes. There is only one way to deal with these young thugs – lock them up and throw away the key!

Here is a longer emotive extract. Consider how it produces its effect and answer the questions that follow.

> Nightingale Wood is surely one of the most beautiful spots in England. A mixed woodland of oak, hazel, ash and wild cherry, it is home to a multitude of animals and birds, from the tiny dormouse to shy but brightly coloured woodpeckers. At dusk, the timid roe deer emerges to feed in nearby fields; as night falls, the badgers snuffle on their age-old paths; and at dawn, an early riser is rewarded by a symphony of birdsong. In spring there are bluebells, and in autumn hazelnuts.
>
> This little Garden of Eden, however, is about to be brutalised – savaged by corporate greed. The sleeping dormouse will be rudely awoken by the ear-splitting sound of chainsaws. Oaks that have stood for centuries will be felled and grubbed up in a matter of minutes. Deer will flee and birdsong will be silenced for ever.
>
> Why is this crime against nature about to occur? So that fat and pampered businessmen can ride their buggies around yet another golf course, and so that Destructive Enterprise Ltd can add another few million to its overflowing bank account!

3 How would you summarise the content and approach of each paragraph?

4 How is the overall effect of the three paragraphs emotive?

5 What phrases in paragraph 1 particularly make the wood seem like a place deserving protection?

6 What phrases in paragraph 2 make what is to happen seem terrible, and how?

7 What phrases in paragraph 3 make the businessmen seem undeserving, and why?

8 What phrases in paragraph 3 make Destructive Enterprise Ltd seem undeserving, and why?

How did I do?

- I know that emotive writing is biased writing which attempts to change how the reader feels. ✔
- I know that emotive writing plays on emotions, including sympathy, guilt, fear and anger. ☐
- I know that individual words and phrases can be emotive, as can the overall effect of a passage. ☐

Teacher's tips

When you complete question 1, it may help you to have a dictionary handy. Often, writers make their writing *emotive* by using powerful **adjectives** and **verbs**. Look out for these. For example, think about what the **adjective** *timid* and the **verb** *brutalised* suggest on page 25.

11: A day in the life of . . .

In this unit you will explore:
- how to plan and draft a piece of non-fiction.

Get started

Non-fiction is any writing that is based in reality.

Planning what you write helps you to know *what* to include. Drafting your piece ensures that *how* you write is as good as possible.

Practice

1 Which of the following types of writing are non-fiction and which are fiction?

autobiographical account	detective novel	description of a place someone has visited
Shakespeare play	newspaper article	police report book review
journal	documentary	poem

Challenge

Amy has been asked to write a piece of non-fiction entitled 'A Day in the Life of a Doctor'. Here is a list of events that she recorded on a particular day.

I get up at 6.00 a.m.
I shower and change
I listen to the radio
I make breakfast for myself and my family
My husband takes the children to school on his way to work
I put the answer machine on
I leave the house at 8.00 a.m.
I stop on my way to work to fill the car and buy a newspaper
I arrive at the surgery
I see fifteen patients and phone three
I meet a friend for lunch and take an unwanted gift back to the shop
I phone my mother and arrange to visit at the weekend
I buy some food
I return to the surgery and see ten more patients
I do some filing and note-taking
I head home

2   **a**   Select from the list which of the events you think Amy should include in her article.
      b   Look through the list again and see if there are any points that could be expanded on. Explain what additional details are needed.

c If you draw a spidergram of a doctor's job, you might end up with something like this:

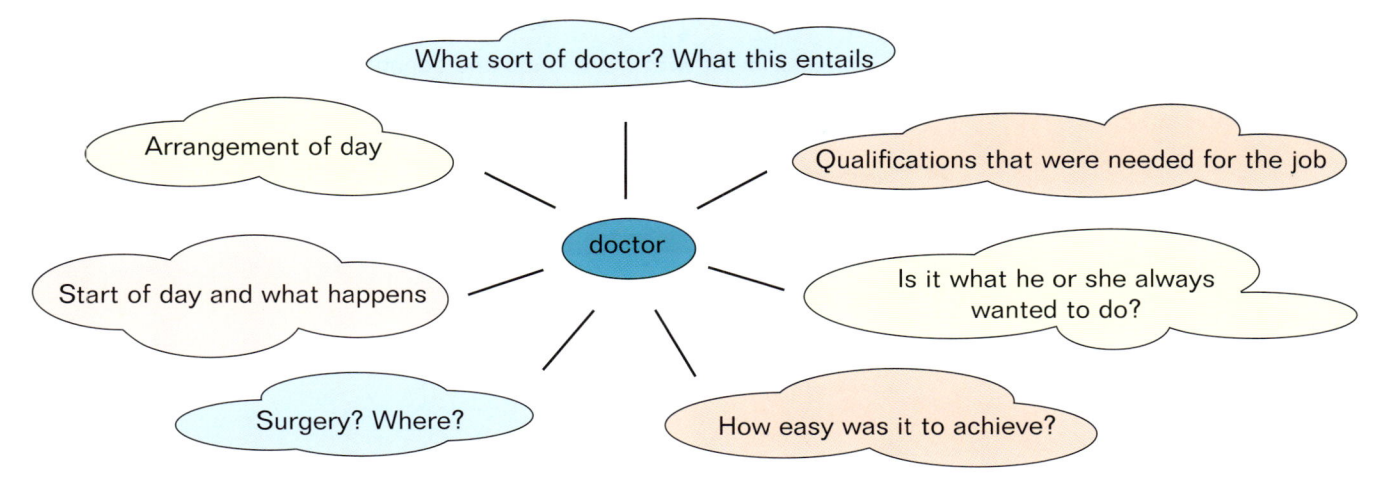

- What sort of doctor? What this entails
- Arrangement of day
- Qualifications that were needed for the job
- doctor
- Start of day and what happens
- Is it what he or she always wanted to do?
- Surgery? Where?
- How easy was it to achieve?

Draw another version of this spidergram, with your own points in each bubble.

3 a Amy tested out a few opening sentences before deciding on her final one. Look at the sentences below and decide which you think works best and why.

- Being a doctor is a tiring job but the rewards are worth it.
- My day starts at 6.00 a.m. when I wake up to the sound of my alarm clock.
- When I was six I wanted to be a princess, but now that I'm 36 I'm glad I'm a doctor.

b Read the start Amy made to her 'A Day in the Life of a Doctor' below. Consider how you would do this differently. Write down any words or phrases you would change and any details or description that you might add.

> **How did I do?**
>
> I know that writing a good piece of non-fiction takes a lot of research and planning.
>
> I know that *what* and *how* are two key considerations for any writer.

My day starts at 6.00 a.m. when I wake up to the sound of my alarm clock. I drag myself away from the comfort of my bed and into a shower. Ten minutes later and I'm ready to make breakfast for everyone. I've been up twice in the night to see to my two-year-old daughter Hanna who is having difficulty sleeping, but I still manage to seem awake by the time I get to the surgery.

Taking it further

Write out your 'A day in the life of X'. Decide whether you will write it in the first or third person and think of an interesting opening sentence.

Teacher's tips

When you write your **Day in the Life** account, it might help you to use **time connectives** or words/phrases that suggest time, such as: *First; Next; Then; By mid-afternoon.*

12: Poetry experiment

In this unit you will explore:
- the rhythm and rhyme of a poem
- its use of alliteration and onomatopoeia.

Get started

Poets experiment with the sounds and connotations of words and phrases in order to enhance the meaning of their poems.

Practice

Read the words listed below.

> malevolent   brindled   bard   primeval   clan   blotched   leers

1 What does each word mean?

2 Write down any words that spring to mind when you hear the sound of each word.

Challenge

Read Don Marquis' poem 'The Tomcat'.

At midnight in the alley
A tom-cat comes to wail,
And he chants the hate of a million years
As he swings his snaky _____.

Malevolent, bony, brindled,
Tiger and devil and bard,
His eyes are coals from the middle of _____,
And his heart is black and _____.

He twists and _____ and capers
And bares his curved sharp claws,
And he sings to the stars of the jungle nights
Ere cities were, or _____.

Beast from a world primeval,
He and his leaping clan,
When the blotched red moon leers over the roofs
Give voice to their scorn of _____.

He will lie on a rug to-morrow
And lick his silky fur,
And veil the brute in his yellow eyes
And play he's tame, and _____.

But at midnight in the alley
He will crouch again and wail,
And beat the time for his demon's song
With the swing of his _____ _____.

3
  a The poem has a set rhythm and rhyme. Work out what these are.
  b Using the rhythm, rhyme and meaning of the poem, fill in the missing words.
  c There are quite a few effective sounds in the poem. Look for examples of onomatopoeia and alliteration.
  d There are also lots of evil-sounding words and phrases. Make a list of these.

4 a Think of an animal you'd like to write about.
(Hint: if it's a difficult animal to visualise or one you don't know much about, research it. Find a picture of it to help you. Research its habitat and its features. Use the internet or an encyclopedia.)

b Brainstorm at least fifteen words about how this animal looks, sounds, feels, smells, moves and so on. Try to think of effective adjectives and verbs of movement. Maybe even think of a comparison or two to use. For a snake, for example, the word 'slithering' is quite good to describe how it moves, 'hiss' for what it sounds like and 'scaly' for what it looks and feels like. Try to think of words that are onomatopoeic in some way.

5 Once you've got a bank of words, look back at the structure of Don Marquis' 'The Tomcat'. You're going to try to use a steady rhythm and rhyme as he does. You might even want to start in a similar way – with a time of day – and then go on to describe the nature of your animal, its movement, sounds and so on.

An example of a start might be:

> At daybreak in the desert
> A viper comes to hiss
> Its fangs outstretched with forked tongue
> Its poisoned deadly kiss

Taking it further

Here are some suggestions for further reading:

- Read 'Cats no less Liquid than their Shadows' by A.S.J. Tessimond and see if you understand what the poet is saying.
- Read 'Macavity: the Mystery Cat' by T.S. Eliot and discover on which Sherlock Holmes figure Eliot supposedly based his poem.
- Read Terry Pratchett's *The Amazing Maurice and his Educated Rodents*.

How did I do?

☑ I know that you can experiment with language to create certain effects.

☐ I know that some of these effects can be created through rhyme, rhythm, alliteration and onomatopoeia.

Teacher's tips

When you write your poem, try to keep a steady **rhythm** by counting the syllables per line and making sure that these follow the example. Reading your poem out loud as you write it will help you with this and with your **rhyming**.

13: Character building

In this unit you will explore:
- how to create characters that are believable and alive.

Get started

Writers create characters through:

- direct description of a character's appearance
- a character's speech – what he or she says and how
- a character's thoughts, feelings and actions
- other characters' thoughts, feelings and actions.

Practice

1 a Look at the adjectives listed below and brainstorm what each suggests to you.

> burly   judicious   wizened   insipid   coy   eccentric

b Now, look at the verbs listed below and do the same.

> scowled   mumbled   stormed   glided   sprang   sauntered

c Do the same with the adverbs listed below.

> ferociously   languidly   heavily   passionately   deprecatingly

Challenge

Read this extract taken from *My Family and Other Animals* by Gerald Durrell. In it, the author recounts his time in Corfu as a young boy, his family's first effort at hiring a car and their first meeting with Spiro.

'Hoy!' roared the voice, 'why donts yous have someones who can talk your own language?'
  Turning we saw an ancient Dodge parked by the kerb, and behind the wheel sat a short barrel-bodied individual, with ham-like hands and a great leathery, scowling face, surmounted by a jauntily-tilted peaked cap. He opened the door of the car, surged out on to the pavement and waddled across to us. Then he stopped, scowling even more ferociously, and surveyed the group of silent cab drivers.
  'Thems been worrying you?' he asked Mother.
  'No, no,' said Mother untruthfully; 'it was just that we had difficulty understanding them.'
  'Yous wants someones who can talks your own language,' repeated the new arrival; 'thems bastards . . . if yous will excuses the words . . . would swindles their own mothers. Excuses me a minute and I'll fix thems.'
  He turned on the drivers a blast of Greek that almost swept them off their feet. Aggrieved, gesticulating, angry they were herded back to their cars by this extraordinary man. Having given them a final and, it appeared, derogatory blast of Greek, he turned to us again.
  'Wheres yous want to go?' he asked almost truculently.

2. Identify the words in the extract that help to create a vivid impression of Spiro's character. Try to find adjectives, verbs and adverbs.

3. What simile does Durrell use to describe Spiro and what is its effect?

4. How does Durrell make Spiro's character seem real and alive? Look carefully at his speech, for example.

5. Look at the following rewritten section of the passage. The meaning of the paragraph has changed very little, so consider why the original is more effective.

> He turned to the drivers and spoke very loudly to them in Greek. They were angry and waving as he took them back to their cars. Then he spoke a final word to them and turned to us again.

6. Sometimes writers accentuate the characteristics of particular characters by contrasting them with another – they use a *foil*. Look at the two short paragraphs below, which describe the apparently separate characters of Jekyll and Hyde. Identify words in the first and second paragraphs that suggest contrast.

> Mr Hyde was pale and dwarfish, he gave an impression of deformity without any nameable malformation, he had a displeasing smile, he had borne himself to the lawyer with a sort of murderous mixture of timidity and boldness, and he spoke with a husky, whispering and somewhat broken voice; all these were points against him, but not all of these together could explain the hitherto unknown disgust, loathing and fear with which Mr Utterson regarded him.
>
> To this rule Dr Jekyll was no exception; and as he now sat on the opposite side of the fire – a large, well-made, smooth-faced man of fifty, with something of a stylish cast perhaps, but every mark of capacity and kindness – you could see by his looks that he cherished for Mr Utterson a sincere and warm affection.

7. You are now going to create your own character. Brainstorm ideas for this. You need to decide on the gender, age, appearance, personality and background of your character. You may even choose to use a foil to help you. Write your description of this character.

Taking it further

Read *The General Prologue* of Chaucer's *Canterbury Tales* and *The Franklin's Tale* retold in modern prose. Geraldine McCaughrean's version of the tales published by Oxford University Press, or Selina Hastings' adaptation published by Walker Books, are two possibilities.

Read one of Chaucer's original tales and see if you can understand some of it.

Create your own description of a Chaucerian pilgrim.

How did I do?

- I know that writers create characters using a number of devices.
- I know that using direct description and speech helps to create believable characters.
- I know that choice of language is also vital to enlivening a character.

Teacher's tips

Remember, the word **contrast** means difference. When you read the extract from *Dr Jekyll and Mr Hyde*, you may need a dictionary to look up some of the unfamiliar words. This will help you to spot the differences between the way the two characters are described.

14: Creative conflict

In this unit you will explore:
- the different ways in which conflict can enhance your stories.

Get started

Stories have characters and a plot. The plot is made up of a beginning, a middle and an end. To move the plot forward, internal or external conflict is necessary.

Practice

1. Find out what each of the following literary terms means.

   a exposition
   b complication
   c rising action
   d climax
   e falling action
   f resolution

2. You should have discovered that one of the above terms means the point in a story when a conflict is introduced, which helps events in the story to unfold. This conflict can be internal or external. What do you understand by the words 'internal' and 'external'?

Challenge

Read this extract taken from *Noughts and Crosses*. Sephy, a Cross, is faced with a number of questions. She is friends with Callum, a Nought, but this is not permitted in a world where Noughts and Crosses do not mix.

There's a proverb which says, 'Be careful what you wish for, because you might get it!' I never really knew what that meant until now. All those months helping Callum with his work so he'd pass the Heathcroft entrance exam. All those nights wishing on every blazing star that Callum would pass so we could go to the same school together, be in the same class together even. And now it'd all come true.

And it was horrible. Everything was going wrong.

I sighed then sighed again. I couldn't hide in the toilet cubicle forever. And who was I hiding from anyway? I was hiding from all those people who'd been pointing and whispering as I walked past them in the school corridor – but mainly from Callum. After what had happened the previous evening I was afraid to face him. I was so afraid he wouldn't be my friend any more. So if I didn't see him I could pretend that nothing between us had changed. But I couldn't sit on the toilet lid forever. The bell rang for the end of breaktime. I stood up and took a deep breath.

'OK . . . Here goes . . .' I muttered to myself.

I drew back the bolt and opened the cubicle door. I was just stepping out of the cubicle when it happened. Lola, Joanne and Dionee from Mrs Watson's class in the year above mine pushed me back into the cubicle and crowded in after me.

'We want to have a word with you,' Lola began.

3 What internal conflict is Sephy facing? Find words and phrases in the text that suggest this conflict.

4 What external conflict does Sephy encounter?

5 What is the effect of using the first person here?

6 Think of a situation in which a character encounters an internal conflict which threatens him or her in some way. Then use this situation as a basis for a short story.
(Hint: writing in the first person is a useful tool when you portray internal conflicts.)

For example:

> I didn't know what to do. How was I ever going to explain what I'd done? My head was racing with all the possible scenarios. I could see it now – Mum's shocked expression and Dad's blank face . . .

7 Think of a situation in which a character faces an external conflict – someone or something that stands in this character's way and prevents him or her from achieving a dream or goal.

8 Malorie Blackman, the author of *Noughts and Crosses*, divides her book into chapters alternately narrated by Sephy and Callum. Write about an incident involving an external conflict but do this from two different points of view – using two different first person narrators.

Taking it further

Read some of the short stories in *From Beginning to End* by Mike Royston. Look at how some of the writers use multiple narrators to show the internal conflicts each character faces and the different approaches they have to external conflicts.

Develop a novella in which you write in separate voices in each chapter to show the way two characters approach a situation.

How did I do?

I know that conflict is central to the movement of plot. ☐

I know that a conflict can be internal or external to a character. ☐

I know that when conflict is included in a story, the choice of viewpoint can enhance the reader's understanding. ☐

Teacher's tips

As this unit is all about conflicts, it might help you to brainstorm a list of all the different words that spring to mind when you hear the word *conflict*.

15: Descriptive delight

In this unit you will explore:
- how to describe a remembered scene.

Get started

Writers select words carefully to create an effective description. Descriptive writing is most vivid when writers refer to senses and employ devices like alliteration and imagery. Writing is most direct when finite verbs are used.

Practice

1 a Look at each group of words listed below and link each with a particular location.

- traffic lights, pedestrian crossing, car horns
- music, dance floor, strobe lighting
- desks, photocopiers, ringing telephones
- check-in desk, tannoy, arrivals board
- candyfloss, merry-go-round, big top

b Write down some adjectives to describe each of the words listed above. Make your adjectives specific to the senses, so refer to sight, sound, touch and smell. For example, you might describe the traffic lights as gleaming or flashing.

Challenge

Read the extracts below. They are taken from Dylan Thomas' *Holiday Memory*.

August Bank Holiday – a tune on an ice-cream cornet. A slap of sea and a tickle of sand. A fanfare of sunshades opening. A wince and whinny of bathers dancing into deceptive water. A tuck of dresses. A rolling of trousers. A compromise of paddlers. A sunburn of girls and a lark of boys. A silent hullabaloo of balloons.
　I remember the sea telling lies in a shell held to my ear for a whole harmonious, hollow minute by a small, wet girl in an enormous bathing suit marked Corporation Property.
　I remember sharing the last of my moist buns with a boy and a lion. Tawny and savage, with cruel nails and rapacious mouth, the little boy tore and devoured. Wild as seedcake, ferocious as a hearthrug, the depressed and verminous lion nibbled like a mouse at his half a bun and hiccupped in the sad dusk of his cage.

Children all day capered or squealed by the glazed or bashing sea, and the steam-organ wheezed its waltzes in the threadbare playground and the waste lot, where the dodgems dodged, behind the pickle factory.
　And mothers loudly warned their proud pink daughters or sons to put that jellyfish down; and fathers spread newspapers over their faces; and sandfleas hopped on the picnic lettuce; and someone had forgotten the salt.

2
  a Make a list of words from the extracts that refer to the different senses. For example, the word 'tune' is specific to hearing.
  b Identify any examples of alliteration or onomatopoeia.
  c Write down any metaphors or similes that you can spot.
  d List all the past tense action verbs you can spot.

3 You are now going to write a description of somewhere you have visited.

  a Think of a place you have visited that you distinctly remember. Make a list of the objects, buildings and people that were there. (Hint: if you cannot remember the scene well, dig out an old photograph and use that to remind you.)
  b Now, write down some adjectives that you could use to describe your list of words.
  c Write down some words that refer to the different senses and that could be used in your description.
  d Write down some interesting comparisons – similes or metaphors.
  e Now, write your description. You could start it like Dylan Thomas' *Holiday Memory* with a reference to a specific day. Then move on to describe your surroundings. (Thomas doesn't write in full sentences but chooses to bombard us with images. You could do the same.)
  An example might be:

> Notting Hill Carnival – a flurry of turquoise and emerald. The blare of a loudspeaker and the thump of a drum. The fan of a butterfly costume, golden and delicate. It sways from side to side, glittering sequins that sparkle like cut glass, blinding me.

You could even write it in the present tense and include yourself in the description. Imagine yourself walking through the scene.

Taking it further

Read some of Dylan Thomas' descriptive poems, like 'Especially when the October wind' or 'We lying by seasand'. Also, read the opening to his famous play *Under Milk Wood.*

Experiment with the sounds of your own work by writing a poem or the opening of a play in which you describe a setting.

How did I do?

✓ I know that writers can delight readers through description. ☐

I know that vivid descriptions can be created through careful selection of vocabulary and images. ☐

Teacher's tips

In case you've forgotten, **onomatopoeia** is when the sound of a word echoes its meaning the way that a *buzzing* bee does. Unit 5 and Unit 4 should help you remember some of the other literary terms used in this unit.

16: Roving reporter

In this unit you will explore:
- bias – a leaning towards one point of view over another
- how to write newspaper articles with different biases.

Get started

Articles address the 5Ws and 1H: Who? What? Where? When? Why? and How?

The bias of an article will depend on its purpose and audience. The style and layout of an article will depend on whether it is from a tabloid or broadsheet paper.

Practice

1. Look at the sentences below and decide which is biased and which is not.

   a. The drunken yob, a typical football hooligan, was hostile and rude.
   b. The man, who was wearing a Manchester United top, seemed to have drunk a lot and was speaking loudly and pointing his finger at me.

2. Identify the words that make one sentence sound biased and the other more factual.

3. Look at the list of features below. Decide whether you think they belong in a tabloid or broadsheet newspaper.

| short paragraphs | colour pictures | lots of detail | stories about celebrities and football stars |
| few pictures | long articles | | |

Challenge

Read this fictional article.

The Minister for Education spoke yesterday about his new bill to increase the amount of time secondary-aged children spend on homework. They already spend a mighty seven hours a week on homework, and this new bill will see this increase to an even mightier ten hours. This comes after months of speculation from the opposing side. Marsha Gates, shadow Education Minister, said that this new suggestion by the government was 'nothing short of ludicrous. Our children already spend too much of their time indoors. Whatever happened to fresh air?'

As of September, all students in Years 7 to 11 will receive at least two hours of homework a week from English, Maths and Science with the remaining four hours being split amongst the other subjects. Despite the minister's insistence that children need this stimulation, psychologists have proven that such pressure on students causes depression and anxiety. With no time left to enjoy themselves, Britain's children are destined not only to become clinically obese but also anxious and depressed couch potatoes.

4 Summarise what the article is about.

5 What is the reported *fact* in the article?

6 What is the reported *opinion* in the article?

The balance of fact and opinion in an article is an indication of its purpose. If there are a lot of opinions and few facts the writer is probably trying to influence your views and opinions. If there are many facts and few opinions, then the writer is more likely to be informing you about an event. Two articles may approach the same event in completely different ways depending on their purpose.

7 What do you think the writer's purpose is in this article?

8 Look at the writer's use of quotations. How does this support the writer's purpose?

Other devices that writers can use to influence readers' opinions are exaggeration and understatement.

9 Look at the following paragraphs and decide which is exaggerated and which understated.

a The traffic ground to a halt and the whole of London was brought to a complete standstill. For over two hours, time froze.

b The prince's abduction of his cousins is a small setback for the royal family. 'Usual teenage antics,' said his father. 'A temporary situation which will be remedied easily.'

Taking it further
Buy copies of the *Guardian* and the *Mirror*. See if you can find two articles about the same subject but written differently.

A writer's bias is obvious when you look at the balance of fact and opinion and the use of exaggeration and understatement. More obviously biased articles tend to be found in tabloid papers.

Read summaries of Chapters 1 and 2 of George Orwell's novel *Animal Farm* (can be found at www.online-literature.com/orwell/animalfarm). In these chapters, the animals of Manor Farm rebel against Farmer Jones and take over the farm because of his mistreatment of them.

10 Write two contrasting tabloid newspaper articles about the takeover of the farm – one for the *Animal Gazette* and the other for *The Star* (the humans' paper). The animals will clearly depict Mr Jones as a villain and the takeover as a victory for animals, and the humans will do the opposite.

11 Write an article about the takeover for a broadsheet paper. The article should be objective and informative.

How did I do?

- I know that when writing articles, reporters consider their purpose and audience.
- I know that bias can be created through the selection of material, the choice of language and deliberate exaggeration or understatement.
- I know that the style and layout of an article will depend on whether it is written for a tabloid or broadsheet paper.

Teacher's tips
Understatement is the opposite of **exaggeration**. If you understate something you play it down and make it sound less important, but if you exaggerate you play it up and make it sound really important.

17: Insider report

In this unit you will explore:
- reports – documents that provide information
- how to write a report.

Get started

Reports are formal documents based on research, evaluations and recommendations. The language used is impartial and objective, not personal and opinionated. Evidence is given for any statements made in a report.

Practice

1. Decide which of these statements sound as if they belong in a report and which do not.

   a. The man was crossing the road when a witness observed that a car struck him.
   b. The cruelty inflicted upon animals cannot be allowed to continue.
   c. The room's contents were spread across it in apparent disarray.

Challenge

Read the following poem called 'Timothy Winters', which the poet Charles Causley based on a real boy.

Timothy Winters comes to school
With eyes as wide as a football-pool,
Ears like bombs and teeth like splinters:
A blitz of a boy is Timothy Winters.

His belly is white, his neck is dark,
And his hair is an exclamation-mark.
His clothes are enough to scare a crow
And through his britches the blue winds blow.

When teacher talks he won't hear a word
And he shoots down dead the arithmetic-bird,
He licks the pattern off his plate
And he's not even heard of the Welfare State.

Timothy Winters has bloody feet
And he lives in a house on Suez Street,
He sleeps in a sack on the kitchen floor
And they say there aren't boys like him anymore.

Old Man Winters likes his beer
And his missus ran off with a bombardier,
Grandma sits in the grate with a gin
And Timothy's dosed with an aspirin.

The welfare Worker lies awake
But the law's as tricky as a ten-foot snake,
So Timothy Winters drinks his cup
And slowly goes on growing up.

At Morning Prayers the Master helves
For children less fortunate than ourselves,
And the loudest response in the room is when
Timothy Winters roars "Amen!"

So come one angel, come on ten
Timothy Winters says "Amen
Amen amen amen amen."
Timothy Winters, Lord. Amen.

2. What impression do you gain of Timothy and his home?

3. Timothy's appearance is compared to things. Explain what each simile or metaphor suggests about Timothy.

4 What evidence can you find to suggest that Timothy is poor and neglected?

5 Why is the law compared to a ten-foot snake?

6 Why do you think the poem ends with the word Amen?

7 Imagine that you are the welfare worker who is trying to get Timothy removed from his family and placed in a caring home. You have to write a report explaining the situation at his current home and making recommendations for improvements.

You need to include information about Timothy's age, where he lives, his family background and the situation at home that suggests improvements need to be made. Use the poem to help you, but make up some details yourself. Look at the format of the report outlined below and use this.

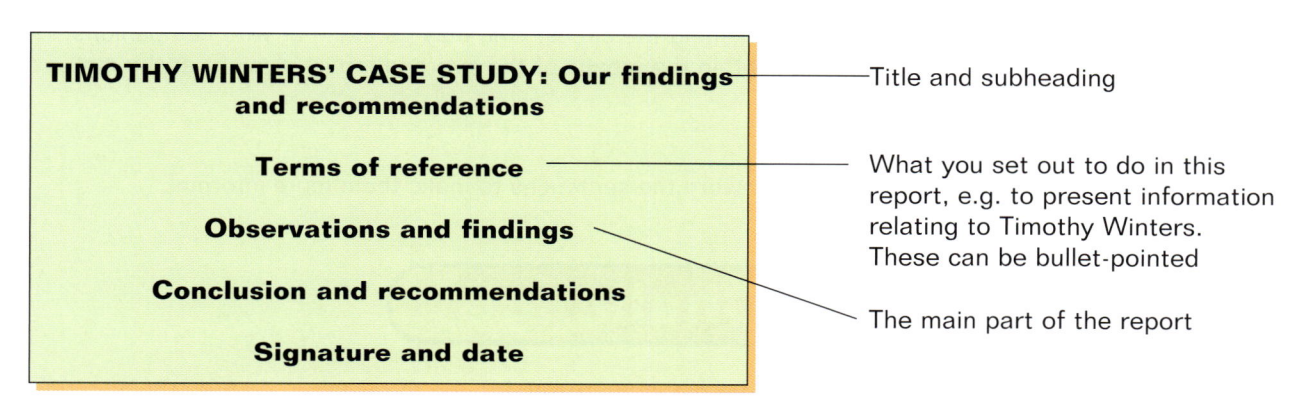

TIMOTHY WINTERS' CASE STUDY: Our findings and recommendations	Title and subheading
Terms of reference	What you set out to do in this report, e.g. to present information relating to Timothy Winters. These can be bullet-pointed
Observations and findings	
Conclusion and recommendations	The main part of the report
Signature and date	

Your main section could start:

Timothy Winters is a twelve-year-old boy who lives with his father and grandmother in Suez Street. His mother left the family home two years ago leaving Timothy to be cared for by his . . .

Taking it further

Imagine that some precious jewels have been stolen from a rich household. You are a police officer called to the scene to investigate. Write your police report.

How did I do?

- I know that reports are factual documents. ☐
- I know that reports must use formal, impartial language. ☐

Teacher's tips

When you **Take it further** you will need to think in detail about the events. How were the police made aware of the burglary? What evidence was found at the scene? Was there any evidence of forced entry to the premises? Are there any suspects/witnesses?

18: Independent research

In this unit you will explore:
- pursuing your purpose
- sources for different types of information
- reliability of information.

Get started

When researching on your own, keep in mind exactly why you need the information. You should also think about the best places to look for different types of information, and how reliable different sources are.

Practice

Much of the more reliable information you find will be written in a *formal* tone. This is the kind of tone in which you might speak to your head teacher. If speaking to a friend, you would probably be more *informal*.

1 What words and phrases make the following sentences formal?

> Many people find considerable enjoyment in visiting the circus. One may go alone or with companions. The charge is usually not excessive, and is well within the means of the average family. A night at the circus can be an extremely amusing diversion.

2 Reword the sentences to make them more informal.

Challenge

3 Here are some topics for you to research. Answer the questions that follow for each topic.

   a Medieval church architecture
   b The career of Leonardo da Vinci
   c What the area you live in was like 200 years ago
   d Egyptian mummies
   e Dolphins

- Why might you need this information (other than for writing a school essay)?
- What questions would you expect to have answered? Think of at least four for each topic.
- Where would you look for the information?
- Under what headings in a library would you expect to find information on the topic?

You will sometimes find contradictory information in different sources. If so, you may need to look for the information in other places and find out what the majority of sources say on the subject.

4 Read the passages below and make a list of ways in which they contradict each other.

Shakespeare's life – passage 1

Shakespeare was the son of a glovemaker, but he received what – for the time – was a reasonable education: he went to Stratford Grammar School, where he learned Latin, logic and history. We do not know exactly when and why William moved to London, but by 1592 he was beginning to gain a reputation as a playwright. His theatrical career was interrupted by an outbreak of smallpox, during which time the theatres were shut. Fortunately, Shakespeare was supported by the wealthy Earl of Salisbury. At this time, Shakespeare wrote some fine poetry, including many sonnets. By 1594 he was back in the theatre, this time as one of The Lord Chamberlain's Men. Shakespeare married a woman much younger than himself, Anne, and had two daughters and a son, Hamnet, who died of plague. Shakespeare himself outlived Queen Elizabeth I – for whom his plays were performed, and died in 1513. He had written 154 plays and 38 sonnets. He is known throughout the world.

Shakespeare's life – passage 2

Shakespeare's success is at least partly the result of his ability to write for all levels of society. Perhaps this is because he was the son of a humble farm worker, yet came to rub shoulders with great men such as the Earl of Southampton. It is also an important factor that he had a classical university education, learning Greek and geography, both of which influenced many of his plays. He was born in Warwickshire, but at some point moved to London, perhaps to escape an accusation of poaching deer. By 1590 he was writing plays, though this was interrupted when the theatres were closed owing to an outbreak of plague. During this time, he was supported by his patron, the Earl of Southampton, and wrote a number of sonnets. By 1595 he was back in the theatre. Shakespeare married Anne, who was older than him. The couple had four children, one of whom, Hamlet, died of the Black Death. Shakespeare lived into the reign of James I, for whom his plays were performed. He died in 1514, having written an astonishing 38 plays and 154 sonnets. He is known worldwide.

Taking it further

Check the information in both passages and write your own account of Shakespeare's life using the correct information and any interesting facts that you discover for yourself.

How did I do?

- I know that it is important to consider what you need information for.
- I know that certain sources are better for certain types of information.
- I know that some sources are more reliable than others.

Teacher's tips

There are many places you can get information for **research** purposes. A library will have books that include biographies, autobiographies and encyclopaedias to name a few. The internet is a rich source of information but you always need to verify whether the information is accurate.

19: Themes

In this unit you will explore:
- what themes are
- how a theme may be handled in different ways
- the themes that writers write about.

Get started

Themes are the ideas that are explored in a text – for example, the power of love, or the evil of racism. Writers may set out to write about a theme, or it may emerge as they write. Either way, different writers tackle the same theme in different ways.

Practice

Sometimes a theme may be represented by a *symbol* in the text – a thing that broadly represents the idea. For example, hatred could be represented by a gun or a dagger – but these items could also be symbols for other themes.

1. Match the objects below with the themes they might symbolise. Explain your choice.

Symbolic object	Theme
sword	truth
wall	knowledge
unicorn	resistance to oppression
pen	the mystery of the universe
fist	hate
mountains	magic
whale	divided communities

Challenge

Read the passage below, from *Holes* by Louis Sachar, and answer the questions that follow.

'Tell me what you learned yesterday,' said the Warden. 'Surely you can remember that.'

Zero said nothing.

Mr Pendanski laughed. He picked up a shovel and said, 'You might as well try to teach this shovel to read! It's got more brains than Zero.'

'The "at" sound,' said Zero.

'The "at" sound,' repeated the Warden. 'Well then, tell me, what does c - a - t spell?'

Zero glanced around uneasily.

Stanley knew he knew the answer. Zero just didn't like answering questions.

'Cat,' Zero said.

Mr Pendanski clapped his hands. 'Bravo! Bravo! The boy's a genius!'

'F - a - t?' asked the Warden.

Zero thought a moment.

Stanley hadn't taught him the 'f' sound yet.

'Eff,' Zero whispered. 'Eff - at. Fat.'

'How about h - a - t?' asked the Warden.

Stanley hadn't taught him the 'h' sound either.

Zero concentrated hard, then said, 'Chat.'

All the counselors laughed.

'He's a genius, all right!' said Mr Pendanski. 'He's so stupid, he doesn't even know he's stupid.'

2 What do you think of Mr Pedanski's attitude towards the boy Zero?

3 How does Stanley's attitude compare with this?

4 What theme or themes do you think the author is exploring here?

5 What do you think the author is saying about this theme?

Read the passage below, from *Hard Times* by Charles Dickens, and answer the questions. In the passage a teacher, Mr Gradgrind, is testing the knowledge of a new pupil, Sissy Jupe, whose father trains horses.

> '. . . Give me your definition of a horse.'
>
> (Sissy Jupe thrown into the greatest alarm by this demand.)
>
> 'Girl number twenty unable to define a horse!' said Mr. Gradgrind, for the general behoof of all the little pitchers. 'Girl number twenty possessed of no facts, in reference to one of the commonest of animals! Some boy's definition of a horse. Bitzer, yours.' . . .
>
> 'Bitzer,' said Thomas Gradgrind. 'Your definition of a horse.'
>
> 'Quadruped. Graminivorous. Forty teeth, namely twenty-four grinders, four eye-teeth, and twelve incisive. Sheds coat in the spring; in marshy countries, sheds hoofs, too. Hoofs hard, but requiring to be shod with iron. Age known by marks in mouth.'
>
> Thus (and much more) Bitzer.
>
> 'Now girl number twenty,' said Mr. Gradgrind. 'You know what a horse is.'

6 What do you think of the way Gradgrind treats Sissy?

7 What theme or themes do you think Dickens is exploring here?

8 What theme do the two passages have in common?

9 What different aspects of this theme are the two authors interested in? (Hint: is Zero really too stupid to learn? Does Sissy really know nothing about horses? Does Bitzer's definition say all there is to know about horses?)

Taking it further

Think of novels, plays and poems you have read. Make a list or spidergram of themes that a writer could explore.

How did I do?

I know that themes are the ideas or topics that an author explores in a text. ✓

I know that writers can explore a theme in different ways, focusing on different aspects of it.

I know that writers explore the themes that have interested people for centuries.

Teacher's tips

To understand what a theme is, it may help you to think about films or programmes you have watched. After watching them what idea were you left thinking about? Sometimes writers and film-makers use symbols to communicate their themes to the audience.

20: Fact, opinion and bias

In this unit you will explore:
- what facts, opinions and bias are
- how writers use all three
- what bias is and how it can be deliberate or accidental.

Get started

Facts are things that are generally accepted to be true and which can be proven.
Example: *Custard contains more calories than cauliflower.*

Opinions are personal viewpoints, which are neither wrong nor right.
Example: *Custard should be banned from school dinner menus.*

Bias is an attitude that makes someone present facts unfairly, encouraging readers to interpret them in one way rather than another.
Example: *Chelsea's heroic play forced a lacklustre Sheffield to a goalless draw.*

Practice

One example of bias in writing is the *ironic* use of quotation marks to tell readers not to take a word or phrase at face value.
Example: *The Minister's 'policy' is actually just a mess of half-formed ideas.*

1 What is implied (suggested) by the quotation marks in the following sentences?

   a I was 'educated' at Cadwallader Comprehensive.
   b My 'home' at the time was a shop doorway.
   c My parents tried to cheer me up with a 'surprise' party.

Challenge

2 Divide the following statements into fact and opinion.

   a A goldfish has a four-second memory span.
   b A goldfish's life is of less value than that of a human.
   c Everest is the highest mountain in the world.
   d Polar bears live in the northern hemisphere.
   e Boys are more intelligent than girls.
   f People used to think that the Sun went round the Earth.

3 Things we think of as facts may one day prove to be wrong. However, this does not make them opinions: they are still factual statements. Match up the half-sentences below to turn them from confused factual statements into correct facts.

   a Gorillas like to   impersonate a police officer.
   b Elephants   have excellent ball control.
   c Mickey Mouse is   President of the United States.
   d It is against the law to   eat large quantities of fruit.
   e Abraham Lincoln was   a lovable cartoon character.
   f Professional footballers   can spray themselves using their trunks.

44

4 Read the two newspaper articles below and comment on:

- how they both use the same facts in biased ways
- which article supports the Prime Minister
- which phrases reveal particular bias.

> The Prime Minister today tried to explain away figures showing that street crime is now out of control. Reported muggings have massively increased over the last five years, and there were 2,305 unsolved muggings last month alone. Figures would be worse, but many people now stay at home for fear of muggers, and often do not bother to report crimes.

> The Prime Minister has welcomed figures showing increased public confidence in the police. The public now considers 80 per cent of street crimes worth reporting and arrests have increased. Out of 4,000 street crimes last month – a three-month low – a mere 2,305 remain unsolved. Figures also showed that people now felt more secure in their homes.

5 When you think you have correctly paired the half-sentences in question 3, make up one opinion on each subject.
Example: *We should all adopt an elephant.*

6 Watch two news broadcasts shown on television on the same day but on different channels. Ideally watch one and record another at the same time. Make a table to show:

- what topics each channel covers
- the order of topics and length of time given to each (showing how important each topic is considered to be)
- any possible bias you notice in presentation, such as how someone is described; for example, 'The *confused* Prime Minister stated . . .'.

Taking it further

Buy two newspapers with differing political views, or visit their websites, and see how they have dealt with the same political news story. Identify differences. You could try, for example, comparing the *Guardian* and the *Daily Telegraph*.

How did I do?

- I know that facts are generally considered to be true, though they may be wrong.
- I know that opinions are viewpoints, and are therefore neither right nor wrong.
- I know that bias is a one-sided representation of facts.

Teacher's tips

You may find work covered in Unit 16 helpful when you complete the work here. Look back at Unit 16 and compare your responses.

21: Irony and satire

In this unit you will explore:
- what irony and satire are
- how writers use them
- how satirical fiction presents a viewpoint.

Get started

Irony is like sarcasm but more subtle. Being sarcastic means sneering at someone or something by saying the opposite of what one really thinks. In Unit 19, Mr Pendanski is being sarcastic when he says 'Bravo! Bravo! The boy's a genius!'. He actually means that the boy is stupid.

Here is an example of writing that is ironic but not sarcastic.

> When I saw the 9.15 express train to Bagshot hurtling towards me, I considered my options carefully. I could write a strongly worded letter of complaint to the appropriate authorities, I could congratulate the driver on his punctuality, or I could finally benefit from my life assurance.

This is ironic because the narrator's careful, formal style is at odds with his situation – and he will not *benefit* much if hit by a train!

Another kind of irony is when something happens that seems particularly inappropriate or unlucky; for example, if someone drives off a cliff when trying to read a road sign like the one below.

> Danger: keep your distance!

Satire uses ironic humour to criticise a powerful person, a political system, society or an institution. Novels, plays, poems and TV shows can be satirical.

Practice

The *tone* of a piece of writing reveals the writer's attitude towards the subject and towards readers.

1. Describe the tone of the following sentences and explain how this tone is achieved.

   a Hi, guys! Seems like a million years since we hung out. How's it goin'?
   b We regret to inform you that the company will no longer require your services.
   c While I have the greatest respect for the President, his inability to think and chew gum at the same time could be considered a disadvantage.
   d Garstang at once enfolded the trembling Amelia in his manly arms. 'Oh, Garstang!' she sighed . . .

Challenge

The passage below is from George Orwell's novel *Animal Farm*, which satirises the way in which the ideals of the Russian Revolution were twisted by the new leaders. The leaders are represented by pigs.

> All the pigs were in full agreement on this point, even Snowball and Napoleon. Squealer was sent to make the necessary explanations to the others.
>
> 'Comrades!' he cried. 'You do not imagine, I hope, that we pigs are doing this in a spirit of selfishness and privilege? Many of us actually dislike milk and apples. I dislike them myself. Our sole object in taking these things is to preserve our health. Milk and apples (this has been proved by Science, comrades) contain substances absolutely necessary to the well-being of a pig. We pigs are brainworkers. The whole management and organisation of this farm depend on us. Day and night we are watching over your welfare. It is for *your* sake that we drink that milk and eat those apples. Do you know what would happen if we pigs failed in our duty? Jones would come back! Yes, Jones would come back! Surely, comrades,' cried Squealer almost pleadingly, skipping from side to side and whisking his tail, 'surely there is no one among you who wants to see Jones come back?'

2. How does the tone of the first paragraph avoid making the criticism too obvious?

3. What proof does Squealer offer that the pigs are not being selfish?

4. How does Squealer use 'Science'?

5. What fear does Squealer use to ensure that the animals are persuaded?

6. How does Orwell make Squealer look ridiculous?

7. How successful do you think this passage is as satire?

8. In *Animal Farm*, the pigs eventually start to do business with the local human farmers – who represent the leaders of non-Communist countries. What do you think is the meaning of the final paragraph (below), in which the animals see the pigs and farmers arguing over a game of cards?

How did I do?

- I know that one type of irony is stating the opposite of what one really means.
- I know that another type of irony is something happening which seems particularly inappropriate or unlucky.
- I know that satire criticises something or someone through humour and ridicule.

> Twelve voices were shouting in anger, and they were all alike. No question, now, what had happened to the faces of the pigs. The creatures outside looked from pig to man, and from man to pig, and from pig to man again: but already it was impossible to say which was which.

Teacher's tips

If you find question 8 difficult, it may help you to have some background knowledge about **Animal Farm** and to read a summary of the novel. You will probably be able to find this information on the internet if you do a search.

22: Structure: the shape of a text

In this unit you will explore:
- structure in a text
- the ways in which texts are usually structured
- why authors use structure.

Get started

All texts have a structure, often building up to a climax. A short story often includes a twist or complication. A well structured text leaves the reader with a sense of *resolution*, with mysteries unravelled and tensions relaxed in a satisfying way.

Practice

1 Turn each of the following sentences into shorter ones. The first has been started for you.

a Standing as far forward as I could, and holding the rod away from the trees, I tried to cast my tackle into the centre of the stream, where I might find a fish.
- I stood as far forward as I could.
- I held the rod away from the trees.

b She was beautiful and, more important, she was brave, both of which are desirable features in a trapeze artist.

c Entering the room with an attempt at dignity, I trod on a toy train – abandoned by Ben – and, clownlike, skidded across the floor before landing in a heap.

Challenge

The opening

Read the opening of Richard Connell's short story 'The Most Dangerous Game', and then answer the questions that follow.

'Off there to the right – somewhere – is a large island,' said Whitney. 'It's rather a mystery –'
   'What island is it?' Rainsford asked.
   'The old charts call it "Ship-Trap Island",' Whitney replied. 'A suggestive name, isn't it? Sailors have a curious dread of the place. I don't know why. Some superstition –'
   'Can't see it,' remarked Rainsford, trying to peer through the dank tropical night that was palpable as it pressed its thick warm blackness in upon the yacht.
   'You've good eyes,' said Whitney, with a laugh, 'and I've seen you pick off a moose moving in the brown fall bush at four hundred yards, but even you can't see four miles or so through a moonless Caribbean night.'

2 How does the opening arouse our curiosity?

3 What is the men's mood at this point, and how do we know?

4 Why do you think the writer shows the men in this mood?

5 What key facts do we learn?

The development

Rainsford hears shots on the island. Read what happens next and answer the questions that follow.

> He leaped upon the rail and balanced himself there, to get greater elevation; his pipe, striking a rope, was knocked from his mouth. He lunged for it; a short, hoarse cry came from his lips as he realized he had reached too far and had lost his balance. The cry was pinched off short as the blood-warm waters of the Caribbean Sea closed over his head.

6 How does the mood change, and why?

7 How might the description of the water foreshadow what is to come?

The twist

Rainsford swims to shore and finds his way through the jungle to a house whose owner, General Zaroff, is a keen hunter and a generous host. Over dinner, Zaroff tells Rainsford how he made his hunting more interesting.

> 'I wanted the ideal animal to hunt,' explained the general. 'So I said, "What are the attributes of an ideal quarry?" And the answer was, of course, "It must have courage, cunning, and, above all, it must be able to reason."'
> 'But no animal can reason,' objected Rainsford.
> 'My dear fellow,' said the general, 'there is one that can.'
> 'But you can't mean –' gasped Rainsford.

8 What animal do you think Zaroff might be talking about?

9 What do you think will happen to Rainsford?

The conclusion

The conclusion is given below – all but the last line. Zaroff has dined alone and is going to bed. Guess what has led up to this – and what the final line will reveal.

> 'Rainsford!' screamed the general. 'How in God's name did you get here?'
> 'Swam,' said Rainsford. 'I found it quicker than walking through the jungle.'
> The general sucked in his breath and smiled. 'I congratulate you,' he said. 'You have won the game.'
> Rainsford did not smile. 'I am still a beast at bay,' he said, in a low, hoarse voice. 'Get ready, General Zaroff.'
> The general made one of his deepest bows. 'I see,' he said. 'Splendid! One of us is to furnish a repast for the hounds. The other will sleep in this very excellent bed. On guard, Rainsford.' . . .

Taking it further

Read 'The Most Dangerous Game' online (for example, at www.classicshorts.com) and see if you guessed correctly.

Draw a chart of the structure of the story.

How did I do?

	✓
I know that sentences and texts have structure.	☐
I know that stories involve complications, and usually reach a climax and resolution.	☐

Teacher's tips

Look back at Unit 14 to help you with this unit. Remember, when you answer question 9 you are just writing what you think. There is no right or wrong answer, although you may think there is a likely conclusion to the story.

23: Comparing texts

In this unit you will explore:
- in what ways fiction texts might differ
- why it is useful to compare texts
- how to compare texts.

Get started

Comparing texts highlights the different style choices the authors have made. This is especially true if the texts have something in common, such as similar themes. Texts can differ in many ways, including subject, theme, viewpoint, imagery and sentence length.

Practice

Texts can be compared on a small scale, at sentence level, as well as on a larger scale.

1 What differences in style do you notice about the following passages?

  a I opened the door and entered quietly. There was cigarette smoke in the air. The TV was still on. I caught a glimpse of movement in the mirror opposite. There was someone in the bedroom. I froze.

  b I opened the door and crept in to find a thin cloud of cigarette smoke hanging on the air, and the TV flickering. As I glanced around, a movement in the mirror rooted me to the spot.

Challenge

Read Extract **a**, noticing its content and style. Then answer the questions that follow.

a Susan ran from the gate down to the open moor, but she was hardly at the foot of the mountain when there was a shout, and, looking round, she saw another armed man leap over the wall in pursuit.

But was he a man? There was something wrong in the way of his running. He was quick and lizard-dry over the grass: his legs raked forward in pecking strides, and the knee joint seemed to be reversed, while below the knee the leg was thin, and the feet were taloned.

Susan had a fifty-yard lead, but she was climbing while the other was still on the downward slope. She scrambled upwards, trying to keep some energy in reserve, but she was driven by the need for escape.

A spear sighed over her shoulder, and stood out of the ground. This pursuer was not going to risk closer contact. Susan thought to pluck up the spear and use it against its owner, but she could not bring herself to face him, nor to use it, nor even to touch it. So again and again she ran on, renewing her lead while the spear was retrieved, and watching for the next throw.

(Alan Garner, *The Moon of Gomrath*)

2 How does the second paragraph arouse our curiosity?

3 What sort of verbs are used in the extract and what is their effect?

4 Whose viewpoint is the description from?

5 What metaphor is used in the final paragraph and what is its effect?

6 What other features do you notice about the style?

Now read Extract **b**, featuring a boy on a makeshift snowboard, and answer the questions that follow.

b And then he heard the noise coming up behind him. The scream of at least two – maybe more – engines. Alex looked back over his shoulder. For a moment there was nothing. But then he saw them – black flies swimming into his field of vision. There were two of them, heading his way.

Grief's men were riding specially adapted Yamaha Mountain Max snowmobiles equipped with 700cc triple-cylinder engines. The bikes were flying over the snow on their 141-inch tracks, effortlessly moving five times faster than Alex. The 300-watt headlights had already picked him out. Now the men sped towards him, cutting the distance between them with every second that passed.

Alex leapt forward, diving into the next slope. At the same moment, there was a sudden chatter, a series of distant cracks, and the snow leapt up all around him. Grief's men had machine-guns built into their snowmobiles! Alex yelled as he swooped down the mountainside, barely able to control the sheet of metal under his feet. The makeshift binding was tearing at his ankle. The whole thing was vibrating crazily. He couldn't see. He could only keep going, trying to keep his balance, hoping that the way ahead was clear.

(Anthony Horowitz, *Point Blanc*)

7 Compare the two extracts in terms of:

- the use of verbs
- narrative viewpoint
- how the authors bring the passages to life and create a sense of urgency
- use of metaphor (see first paragraph in Extract **b**).

8 Which extract do you prefer, and why?

Taking it further

Write a short essay comparing the two extracts. Try to mention both in each paragraph you write. Include:

- comment on what sort of book you think each extract comes from
- what sort of reader each is aimed at
- your personal response to each.

Reread a few pages from two novels you have read, and then compare their style.

How did I do?

I know that comparing texts is a good way to identify their styles.

I know that fiction can differ in many ways, depending on the author's choices.

Teacher's tips

Narrative viewpoint is the view from which we see events. A passage may be written in *first person, third person, third person limited* or *omniscient* view points. Try to find out what each of these terms means to help you in this unit. Unit 53 may help.

24: What is context?

In this unit you will explore:
- what the context of a text is
- social and historical context
- literary context.

Get started

The context of a text means the circumstances that influenced the author and helped to make the text what it is. Social and historical context go together. Society influences the author, and society itself changes over time. For example, Shakespeare's plays reflect the fact that women in his time were expected to stay at home and obey their husbands. The literary context of a text is how the author has been influenced by other writers.

Practice

Words have a historical context – how they have evolved from other words, both in English and in the languages from which English has come.

1. The word-ending -*logy* (as in ornithology, the study of birds) comes from the Greek word *logos* (reason, or knowledge). What words can you think of that end like this?

2. The word-ending -*phobia* (as in claustrophobia, the fear of enclosed spaces) comes from the Greek word *phobos* (fear). What words can you think of that end like this?

Challenge

3. Read the following passages, all published in the nineteenth century. Make notes on what they tell us about nineteenth-century British attitudes towards:
   - poor people
   - children
   - schoolgirls
   - religion
   - exploration
   - foreigners.

a They told me of thousands of beautiful fertile islands that had been formed by a small creature called the coral insect, where summer reigned nearly all the year round, – where the trees were laden with a constant harvest of luxuriant fruit, – where the climate was almost perpetually delightful, – yet where, strange to say, men were wild, bloodthirsty savages, excepting in those favoured isles to which the gospel of our Saviour had been conveyed.

(R.M. Ballantyne, *The Coral Island*, 1858)

b 'Please, sir, I want some more.'

The master was a fat, healthy man; but he turned very pale. He gazed in stupefied astonishment on the small rebel for some seconds, and then clung for support to the copper. The assistants were paralysed with wonder; the boys with fear.

'What!' said the master at length, in a faint voice.

'Please, sir,' replied Oliver, 'I want some more.'

The master aimed a blow at Oliver's head with the ladle; pinioned him in his arms; and shrieked aloud for the beadle.

(Charles Dickens, *Oliver Twist*, 1838)

c 'Humility is a Christian grace, and one peculiarly appropriate to the pupils of Lowood; I, therefore, direct that especial care shall be bestowed on its cultivation amongst them. I have studied how best to mortify in them the worldly sentiment of pride; and, only the other day, I had a pleasing proof of my success. My second daughter, Augusta, went with her mama to visit the school, and on her return she exclaimed: 'Oh, dear papa, how quiet and plain all the girls at Lowood look, with their hair combed behind their ears, and their long pinafores, and those little holland pockets outside their frocks – they are almost like poor people's children!'

(Charlotte Brontë, *Jane Eyre*, 1847)

4 Read the passage below, from Shakespeare's *The Merchant of Venice* (1598).

    a What does it tell us about attitudes to Jews in Shakespeare's time?
    b What do you think Shakespeare's own attitude towards Jews was?

He hath disgraced me, and hindered me half a million; laughed at my losses, mocked at my gains, scorned my nation, thwarted my bargains, cooled my friends, heated mine enemies; and what's his reason? I am a Jew. Hath not a Jew eyes? Hath not a Jew hands, organs, dimensions, senses, affections, passions? Fed with the same food, hurt with the same weapons, subject to the same diseases, healed by the same means, warmed and cooled by the same winter and summer, as a Christian is? If you prick us, do we not bleed? If you tickle us, do we not laugh? If you poison us, do we not die? and if you wrong us, shall we not revenge?

(*The Merchant of Venice*, Act 3, scene 1)

How did I do?

- I know that context means the background that influenced the author. ☐
- I know that social and historical context reflects changes in society, such as attitudes towards the poor, women and girls, foreigners and ethnic minorities. ☐

Teacher's tips

You may need to read the passages a few times to understand what they mean, especially as the language may be unfamiliar to you. Once you have read each passage, look out for key words. Use the prompts provided to focus your reading.

25: Genre

In this unit you will explore:
- what genre is
- what different genres there are
- the characteristics of different genres.

Get started

A *genre* is a text, usually fictional, with a particular set of features. Some examples are shown below.

comedy   horror   adventure   satire   romance

science fiction   fantasy   crime

Practice

Tenses are important in fiction. Most fiction is in the past tense, but a few novels are written entirely in the present tense.

1 Read the following passage and suggest what the effect is of using the present tense – and the future tense at the end.

> I climb the ladder carefully and with my heart beating hard, push open the trap door and manoeuvre myself into the loft. Light filters in through a skylight, dimly illuminating a flurry of dust, which slowly settles as I look around. In the corner stands the chest. What will it contain?

Challenge

2 Read the extracts below. Identify which genre listed under Get started each one falls into.

a Jess hurled herself at the car bonnet and, miraculously, managed to cling to a wiper blade. As the car accelerated she felt its 3 litre engine vibrate beneath her. She grasped the other wiper and braced herself against the sleek metal, lurching sideways as the desperate driver swerved repeatedly in an attempt to dislodge her. Through the windscreen she could see his face, twisted in a mask of fury.

b Varg was no ordinary timelord. He had dominion over an entire fleet of Galactigons. He was not going to let the puny earthlings get the better of him! Making his mind up, he fixed his third eye on the cloudy globe of the Galaxeron, and soon began to experience the familiar sense of lightness that always came when he teleported himself to other planets.

c As the moon slid like a blade from behind the chasing clouds, he caught sight of the child moving fast through the broken gravestones. She was half turned away, but seemed to be shivering. Poor thing, he thought. He lost sight of her for a moment in the shade of an ancient yew tree, and when he saw her again, she was much closer. A chill trickled down his spine. She was standing by a newly dug grave, and as she turned, she smiled. He froze . . .

d Whoever had done this job had been smart – very smart. No fingerprints, not a thing disturbed or out of place. A real pro, thought Stonefield admiringly.

'I want DNA on the wineglass, plus the usual snapshots. Check the answerphone. Maybe our friend made a booking.'

'Guv,' began a nervous PC.

'What is it?' snapped Stonefield, his mind already moving on.

'I think you'd better take a look at this . . .'

3 You probably managed to identify the genres, but can you also list what it is in each extract that gives it away? Look for the less obvious signs as well as the obvious ones. Comment on the tone in each passage, the kinds of verbs and adjectives used, and what sort of details are given.

4 Sometimes two genres can be combined. Which two do you think are used in the following extract?

Spegalon, Overlord of Phlebon, Ultimate Authority on the Third Moon of Betelgeuse, owner of the biggest chain of black holes in the entire galaxy, was having a really bad day. The teleporter had malfunctioned, leaving one of his heads hovering in mid-air several metres above his shoulders. True, two heads are better than one, but only when they are in reasonably close contact. Added to that, he had just accidentally obliterated his own grandmother in a time warp. By rights, he shouldn't even exist.

Taking it further

Think about the last two or three novels you have read. What genres do they most easily fit into, and which features influence your decision?

How did I do?

I know that genres are types of writing with particular characteristics. ✓

I know that many novels fit into a particular genre, such as crime or fantasy.

I know that it is also possible for a novel to combine two genres.

Teacher's tips

To answer question 4, look out for key words that suggest a particular genre. Are there any technical words for example? Also consider the effect of the passage on the reader. Does it make you sad or happy? Does it make you laugh?

26: Form in poetry

In this unit you will explore:
- why form is important in poetry
- how form contributes to meaning
- some poetic forms.

Get started

Form in poetry means how a poem is structured. This consists of two main things:

- *metre* – the number and pattern of syllables in the lines, i.e. the *rhythm*
- *rhyme* – if the poem rhymes, the pattern of rhymes, known as the *rhyme scheme*.

Practice

The smallest pronounceable part of a word is called a *syllable*. A poetic metre consists of a set number of syllables, in a particular pattern of *stressed* and *unstressed*. One bit of this pattern – like one link in a chain – is called a *foot*. Think of it walking along!

Read the following line aloud, counting out the 'beats' of its rhythm:

'If music be the food of love, play on.' (Shakespeare, *Twelfth Night*)

You should find it sounds like this:

De-<u>dum</u>, de-<u>dum</u>, de-<u>dum</u>, de-<u>dum</u>, de-<u>dum</u>.

Each 'de-dum' is a 'foot' of one unstressed syllable followed by one stressed one. There are five pairs.

1 Work out the pattern of stressed and unstressed syllables in the following lines:

    a By the shining Big-Sea-Water
    b O what can ail thee, knight-at-arms
    c Like the leaves of the forest when Summer is green

Challenge

Read the extracts below out loud, beating out their rhythm. Then answer the questions that follow.

Without speaking, without pausing,
Kwasind leaped into the river,
Plunged beneath the bubbling surface,
Through the whirlpools chased the beaver,
Followed him among the islands,
Stayed so long beneath the water,
That his terrified companions

Cried, "Alas! good-by to Kwasind!
We shall never more see Kwasind!"
But he reappeared triumphant,
And upon his shining shoulders
Brought the beaver, dead and dripping,
Brought the King of all the Beavers.

(from Henry Longfellow, 'The Song of Hiawatha')

O what can ail thee, knight-at-arms,
   Alone and palely loitering?
The sedge has wither'd from the lake,
   And no birds sing.

O what can ail thee, knight-at-arms!
   So haggard and so woe-begone?
The squirrel's granary is full,
   And the harvest's done.

I see a lily on thy brow
   With anguish moist and fever dew,
And on thy cheeks a fading rose
   Fast withereth too.

(from John Keats, 'La Belle Dame sans Merci')

   The Assyrian came down like the wolf on the fold,
And his cohorts were gleaming in purple and gold;
And the sheen of their spears was like stars on the sea,
When the blue wave rolls nightly on deep Galilee.

   Like the leaves of the forest when Summer is green,
That host with their banners at sunset were seen:
Like the leaves of the forest when Autumn hath blown,
That host on the morrow lay withered and strown.

   For the Angel of Death spread his wings on the blast,
And breathed in the face of the foe as he passed;
And the eyes of the sleepers waxed deadly and chill,
And their hearts but once heaved, and for ever grew still!

(from Lord Byron, 'The Destruction of Sennacherib')

2 How is the rhythm of Longfellow's poem appropriate to its Native American subject?

3 Which poem's rhythm sounds like galloping horses, and why is this appropriate?

4 Which poem has a regular 'ballad' rhythm except for each fourth line – and how does this help to create the mood?

5 Which lines rhyme in Keats's poem?

6 What is the rhyme scheme in Byron's poem and how does it fit the subject?

Some poems are written in an even stricter structure, with a certain number of syllables per line, in a set number of lines.

7 Count the syllables to work out the rules for the following type of poem – a haiku.

> The river in flood
> Muddy brown water racing
> Ducks take a free ride

Taking it further

Search for "Shakespeare" and "sonnet" online. Read one of Shakespeare's sonnets and see if you can work out its form. If you can't work it out, check the Glossary.

How did I do?

✓

- I know that the two most important elements of poetic form are rhythm and rhyme. ☐
- I know that a set rhythmic pattern is called a metre. ☐
- I know that metre and rhyme are used to reinforce meaning. ☐

Teacher's tips

An additional tip for recognising a haiku, aside from its rhythm and number of lines, is the fact that very often haikus are written about some aspect of nature.

27: Planning a character analysis

In this unit you will explore:
- how to plan and draft an essay about a character.

Get started

Writers create characters using various devices, which you can use yourself when planning an essay on a character.

Practice

1 Brainstorm some words that occur to you when you think of a rat.

Challenge

Read the following extract from Roald Dahl's short story 'The Hitchhiker'.

Ahead of me I saw a man thumbing a lift. I touched the brake and brought the car to a stop beside him. I always stopped for hitchhikers. I knew just how it used to feel to be standing on the side of a country road watching the cars go by. I hated the drivers for pretending they didn't see me, especially the ones in big cars with three empty seats. The large expensive cars seldom stopped.

It was always the smaller ones that offered you a lift, or the old rusty ones or the ones that were already crammed full of children and the driver would say, 'I think we can squeeze in one more.'

The hitchhiker poked his head through the open window and said, 'Going to London, guv'nor?'

'Yes,' I said. 'Jump in.'

He got in and I drove on. He was a small ratty-faced man with grey teeth. His eyes were dark and quick and clever, like rat's eyes, and his ears were slightly pointed at the top. He had a cloth cap on his head and he was wearing a greyish-coloured jacket with enormous pockets. The grey jacket, together with the quick eyes and the pointed ears, made him look more than anything like some sort of a huge human rat.

'What part of London are you headed for?' I asked him.

'I'm goin' right through London and out the other side,' he said. 'I'm goin' to Epsom, for the races. It's Derby Day today.'

'So it is,' I said. 'I wish I were going with you. I love betting on horses.'

'I never bet on horses,' he said. 'I don't even watch 'em run. That's a stupid silly business.'

'Then why do you go?' I asked.

He didn't seem to like that question. His little ratty face went absolutely blank and he sat there staring straight ahead at the road, saying nothing.

2 Why does the narrator stop for the hitchhiker?

3 What does this suggest about the narrator's character?

4 Identify any words or phrases from the text that tell us about the hitchhiker's character. Look at what he looks like, what he says, how he speaks and what he does. Also look at what the narrator thinks about him.

5 Draw a table like the one below. Using the information you gathered in question 4, fill it in, making deductions about what the information in the passage shows us about the hitchhiker.

Quotation from the text	What this shows
'Going to London, guv'nor?'	The man is probably a Cockney.

When you write an essay about a character or any piece of literature, you write what is called a critical essay. A critical essay is made up of three sections: an introduction, a main body and a conclusion.

6 Match the definitions below with what you think each of these sections is.

  a This section is made up of several paragraphs, each making a point, providing evidence and following on from the previous paragraph.
  b This section comes at the start of the essay and is made up of one paragraph, which focuses your essay and gives an idea of its main points.
  c This section comes at the end of the essay and is usually one paragraph, which ties up the essay and includes your final comments about the topic.

7 You are going to write an essay answering the question: 'What impression do we gain of the hitchhiker from this passage?'

  a Start by organising your ideas about the hitchhiker. Decide where your ideas will go – which ideas will go in your first paragraph and so on. Think carefully about how you will organise these.
  b Write the first paragraph.
  c Now, write the next few paragraphs with evidence to support your comments.
  d Now write your final paragraph.

This is your draft of the essay. You must now go back and check it for errors in facts, spelling, punctuation and grammar. You should also try to use the best possible English, so reread the essay and try to improve your language.

Taking it further

Read the whole of 'The Hitchhiker' (copies can be found on the internet). Then compare the hitchhiker to the narrator or policeman.

How did I do?

✓

☐ I know that when I read about a character I look at his or her appearance, speech, thoughts and actions.

☐ I know that when I plan an essay about a character I should collect evidence and organise my ideas.

☐ I know that when I draft an essay about a character I should write an introduction, main body and conclusion, and then check my essay.

Teacher's tips

For question 6, decide whether **a** defines an introduction, main body or conclusion. Do the same for the definitions provided in **b** and **c**.

28: Parody party

In this unit you will explore:
- what a parody is
- how to write a parody of a fairy tale.

Get started

A parody is an imitation of something that results in it sometimes becoming humorous and exaggerated. A parody of a fairy tale might set the story in a future world or in modern times or might change it in some other way.

Practice

1. List some well-known fairy tales.

2. How do fairy tales traditionally start and what features do they include?

Challenge

Read the following two sections taken from tales.

Long, long ago, in the winter-time, when the snowflakes were falling like little white feathers from the sky, a beautiful queen sat beside her window, which was framed in black ebony, and stitched. As she worked, she looked sometimes at the falling snow, and so it happened that she pricked her finger with her needle, so that three drops of blood fell upon the snow.

It just so happened that on a frosty morning in December Lady Marbury was sitting at her window, reading her copy of *OK!* magazine and watching the snow drift softly down from the sky. She was so preoccupied with watching the snow and flicking through her magazine so energetically that she gave herself a nasty paper cut. Three ruby red drops of blood fell onto a page and all over a football star's face.

3. Which is a parody and which is an original?

4. Which words and phrases helped you decide which story was an original and which was a parody?

Read the beginning of this well-known fairy tale.

Once upon a time there lived a young girl whose father had remarried after her mother's death. This poor girl, named Cinderella, was treated like a slave by her nasty and wicked stepmother, who praised and loved her two blood daughters. She and they would order Cinderella around.

'Get me this. Do that.'

And nothing was ever good enough. They were always criticising Cinderella and making her sad so that one morning she found herself crying in a corner, when there was a knock at the door.

'Who could this be?' Cinderella thought as she walked towards it. Her lazy stepsisters and stepmother were still in bed and it was part of her household duties to sweep and clean, so as she approached the door her face was covered in dust.

> 'Hello,' said a messenger, who was grandly dressed. 'I have an invitation here for this house to attend a ball at the royal palace.' He handed Cinderella the invitation and turned to leave.
>
> 'A ball,' thought Cinderella, her heart brightening with glee. Little did she know that her wicked stepfamily had no intention of letting her go to any ball, or anywhere for that matter.

5 Write bullet points to summarise the remaining plot.

6 Which of the following devices could be used by writers to create humour?

- exaggeration
- long sentences
- understatement
- situations that seem ridiculous
- short sentences
- word play
- stating the obvious
- detail

Read the beginning of a parody of this Cinderella tale, re-told in modern times.

> Once there was a young girl who lived on the outskirts of London with her stepmother, Marsha, her two stepsisters, Sharon and Tracy, and her father, Doug. Cindy was beautiful and clever. In fact, she was hoping one day to become a solicitor and because of this her stepfamily envied her in every way possible. Sharon and Tracy, despite being ugly in look and character, spent each Saturday at the shops buying Gucci handbags and shoes and looking for rich city bankers to trap. They would poke their long and hairy noses into every nook and cranny they could find in the vain hope that they might come across a tall, dark and handsome, but very stupid, rich man who would marry them. Cindy, on the other hand, had to stay indoors washing their clothes and cleaning the house before sneaking in a couple of hours of reading. It was on one such Saturday that Cindy heard a knock at the door.

7 In what ways is this story a parody?

8 Identify words and phrases that give the tale some humour.

9 Look back at your list of bullet points. Continue this parody or create your own.

How did I do?

- I know that fairy tales are stories for children, which often involve magic. ✔
- I know that a parody uses elements from an original tale and changes these so that they may become humorous, exaggerated, modernised or politically correct.

Taking it further

Read one or two examples of politically correct fairy tales. (Search for "politically correct fairy tale" to find some on the internet.)

Try to write your own version of such a tale.

Teacher's tips

You might want to read the passages to a friend to see which bits cause them to smile or laugh. This may help you to identify the humour.

29: 'The Dream Woman'

In this unit you will explore:
- how to write in the voice of a character from a text.

Get started

Taking on the voice of a character from a text requires you to put yourself in his or her position and to adopt his or her language.

Practice

1. Which of these sentences sound as if they come from a story set in the past?

   a He didn't want to come to the cinema.
   b The servant-girl takes after her misuses.
   c It was nigh on twenty minutes past two.
   d She flicked through the magazine.

2. Which words helped you to make your decisions?

Challenge

Read this extract adapted from Wilkie Collins' short story 'The Dream Woman'. Isaac, a stable hand, is staying at an inn overnight when a strange vision appears to him.

The first sensation of which he was conscious after sinking into slumber was a strange shivering that ran through him suddenly from head to foot, and a dreadful sinking pain at the heart, such as he had never felt before. In one moment he passed from a state of sleep to a state of wakefulness – his eyes wide open – his mental perceptions cleared on a sudden, as if by a miracle.

The candle had burnt down nearly to the last morsel of tallow, but the light in the little room was, for the moment, fair and full.

Between the foot of his bed and the closed door there stood a woman with a knife in her hand, looking at him.

He was stricken speechless with terror, but he did not lose the preternatural clearness of his faculties, and he never took his eyes off the woman. She said not a word as they stared each other in the face, but she began to move slowly toward the left-hand side of the bed.

His eyes followed her. She was a fair, fine woman, with yellowish flaxen hair and light gray eyes, with a droop in the left eyelid. Speechless, with no expression in her face, with no noise following her footfall, she came closer and closer – stopped – and slowly raised the knife. He laid his right arm over his throat to save it; but, as he saw the knife coming down, threw his hand across the bed to the right side, and jerked his body over that way just as the knife descended on the mattress within an inch of his shoulder.

His eyes fixed on her arm and hand as she slowly drew her knife out of the bed: a white, well-shaped arm, with a pretty down lying lightly over the fair skin – a delicate lady's hand, with the crowning beauty of a pink flush under and round the finger nails.

As she approached she raised the knife again and he drew himself away to the left side. She struck, as before, right into the mattress, with a deliberate, perpendicularly-downward action of the arm. His eyes wandered from her to the knife. For the second time, she drew the knife out, concealed it in the wide sleeve of her gown, then stopped by the bedside, watching him. For an instant he saw her standing in that position, then the wick of the spent candle fell over into the socket; the flame diminished to a little blue point, and the room grew dark.

3 What strange feeling woke Isaac?

4 Find some words and phrases that suggest Isaac's fear.

5 Describe what Isaac saw.

When Isaac wakes the landlord of the inn and claims that a woman has tried to kill him, they discover that his bedroom window and door are still locked shut and the mattress into which a knife is supposed to have plunged is untouched. The landlord concludes that the image was a dream and chides Isaac for disturbing the house with his madness. Isaac is disturbed by this and is left to think about the events of the night.

6 You are going to write Isaac's diary entry the next day.

   a First, make a list of the points that you will include – what events will you refer to?
   b Now, think about how Isaac feels and what his thoughts may be. Write down your thoughts.

Read the following two extracts from attempts at diary entries.

> He was upset and could not believe what had happened to him. Who had that woman been and had he imagined her? How could that be true when she had seemed so real to him?

> What vision was this that visited me last night? My discoveries after she had gone told me that she had been nothing more than a figment of my imagination. Yet, I cannot deny what my eyes observed.

7 Which sounds more like a diary entry and why?

8 Which sounds like it is from the same time as 'The Dream Woman' and why?

9 Write Isaac's diary entry. Think carefully about your language as you write.

Taking it further

Read the whole of Wilkie Collins' story (copies can be found on the internet).

Write another diary entry for Isaac at the end of the story.

How did I do?

	✔
I know that when writing the diary entry of a character I should imagine that I am this person.	☐
I know that I should refer to events, thoughts and feelings, and write in the first person.	☐
I know that I should use the language that the character would use.	☐

Teacher's tips

When you write Isaac's diary, imagine yourself at the inn at night, using a quill and writing on parchment paper. Sometimes when you write, you have to draft your ideas a few times before you create your best piece so don't be afraid to do this with your diary entry.

30: Quality not quantity

In this unit you will explore:
- how to write a 250-word short story
- how to write a mini saga (a 50-word story).

Get started

Writing to a set word limit requires you to choose the best words and write with precision.

Practice

1 Look at the pairs of words listed below. What is the difference between the words in each of the pairs?

get – retrieve	see – scrutinise	walk – amble	sad – depressed
red – crimson	hard – coarse	sporty – agile	smelly – fragrant

Challenge

Read the following 250-word story.

May had never seen the sun.
  'It disappeared after the first explosion,' her grandmother said. 'A huge mushroom cloud grew above us; its dust fell down from the sky one piece at a time.' She cast her eyes down. 'To this day, I can still see it – that blanket of dust. I was indoors, the heat so intense my face blistered as sure as if my skin had been fried.'
  May looked up at her grandmother; the scarred skin and vacant eyes stared past her.
  'That blast took the light away.'
  She nodded and stroked her grandmother's hair. 'Took more than that,' May said.
  'That it did. Why your Grandpa, he was a fine man. Head and shoulders above any other. That man was all heart, and your ma . . .'
  A tear traced its way down her cheek.
  'Out of doors when it happened – he and your ma getting into that rust bucket. I'd just waved 'em off and, you, you were just a baby in my arms.' She sighed. 'Forty years, May. It's been forty years – of darkness and cold, and now this.'
  She smiled serenely.
  'I can feel the warmth again, May, and God willing, now, your darkness will end.'
  'Ah, Grandma, I wish you could see it,' May said, taking hold of her grandmother's hand, but just as she did it slipped from hers, and those vacant eyes slid shut.
  May looked at the light in the sky, and back at her grandmother. 'Now our darkness has ended,' she said.

2 What happens in the story?

3 Who are the characters?

4 Identify any words from the story that you think are particularly precise or well chosen and explain why you think this.

5 What do you understand by 'Now our darkness has ended'?

6 Being able to write concisely is a key skill when your word limit is small. Look at the phrases listed below and think of substitute single words.

   a make something sound bigger or better than it is: e_____
   b unnecessarily long winded: v_____
   c can be seen through: t_____
   d make something clearer so that it is understood: c_____
   e draw attention to something: h_____
   f fall over something: t_____

7 Think of your own plot for a short story. Limit yourself to one or two characters and a simple plot based on a haunted house. Write your story. If it runs over 250 words try to make phrases more concise, or cut them completely.

Reduce your 250-word story to 50 words.

Taking it further

Reduce the following 70 words to a 50-word mini saga.

> It was late in the evening. The stars shone down from the sky and the moon beamed down on us. We were driving through the night to the hotel. The car rattled its way along the deserted and dark road. The light beams flickered on and off and the road was eerily quiet. We were approaching a fork in the road when the car spluttered and came to a halt.

How did I do?

✓

I know that in order to write a 250-word short story I have to choose my words carefully.	☐
I know that a mini saga is a 50-word story.	☐
I know that when writing a mini saga, I should limit myself to one or two characters and straightforward action.	☐

Teacher's tips

A trick to removing words in an extended piece of writing is to cut out the adjectives or adverbs and use more precise verbs. For example, rather than writing *The sun shone brightly*, you could write *The sun glowed*.

31: All about me

In this unit you will explore:
- how to write a creative autobiographical account.

Get started

Autobiographical accounts are narrative descriptions about a person's real life written by the person him- or herself. Whilst these accounts are factually true, writers may embellish and exaggerate sections to entertain their readers.

Practice

1. Identify which are facts and which opinions in the following sentences.

   a. It was Tuesday evening.
   b. *X Factor* is an awful show.
   c. The road wound to the left.
   d. The car spluttered to a halt.
   e. Chelsea is the best football team ever.
   f. Tom Cruise is a top actor.

Challenge

Read the following extract taken from Amy Tan's book *The Opposite of Fate*.

After two weeks in Holland, we took a train to Germany and landed in Karlsruhe, where we lived as guests of a U.S. Army chaplain, an old friend of my father's. We attended an American school, where students thought it a fun prank to aim lit Bunsen burners at one another. This, I told my mother, was not the kind of education she had had in mind when she had envisioned us studying abroad. With that, she bought a Volkswagen Beetle and a handbook of English-speaking schools, and off we went, heading south, letting ourselves be guided purely by the twists and turns of European highways.

By such maps of fate, we wound up in Montreux, Switzerland, at the shores of Lake Geneva. In this resort town, my mother quickly found our new home, a fully furnished chalet, complete with cuckoo clock and feather-tick beds, renting for the equivalent of one hundred U.S. dollars a month. The largest room served as living room, dining room, and my brother's bedroom, and its entire length was lined with mullioned windows showcasing a spectacular view of the lake and the Alps. Every day, I would stare at this amazing scenery and wonder how I came to be so lucky. I would then remember that my father and older brother were dead, and that was the reason I was here.

Half a mile from our chalet, down a cobblestone path, lay an international school. It was within eyesight of Château de Chillon, where the dashing Lord Byron was said to have chained himself to write his poetry in religious agony. By happy chance, there were two openings for day students. My mother weighed the benefits of a four-to-one pupil–teacher ratio, the mandatory ski outings as physical education, the private piano lessons and one-to-one drawing classes, the Spanish teacher from Spain, the French teacher from France, and English teachers from England, and decided it was all worth the extravagant cost of six hundred dollars per year.

2 Identify words and sentences from the extract that sound factual (true) and any words or phrases that seem to have been exaggerated or are written to entertain.

3 Write some facts about your own life.

4 Look at the following sentences.

- By such maps of fate, we wound up in Montreux, Switzerland, at the shores of Lake Geneva.
- It ended up that we arrived in Switzerland.

What is the difference between these two sentences?

5 Find some details from the passage that add interest but are not entirely necessary to the factual account.

6 Add interest to your facts from question 3.

7 Amy Tan refers to events, settings, conversations and thoughts. Identify where each of these appears in the passage.

8 Amy Tan uses carefully chosen vocabulary. Select four or five verbs and adjectives that you think are effective and explain why you think this.

9 You are going to write your own autobiographical account, using some of Amy Tan's techniques. Decide on a particular episode from your life on which you will focus.

   a Create a spidergram of ideas related to this episode.

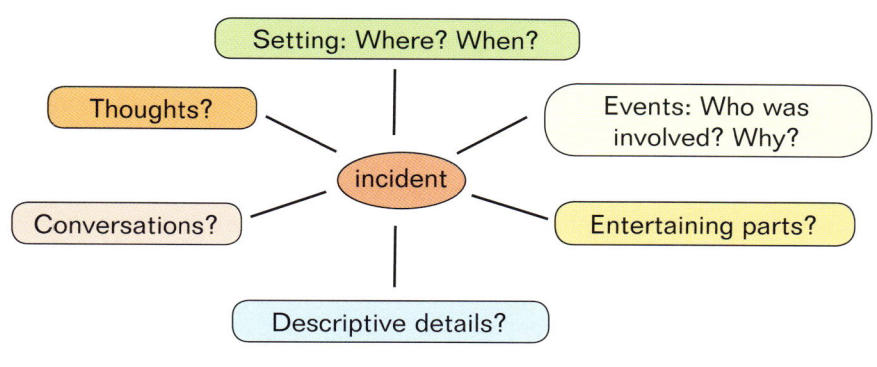

   Spidergram centred on "incident" with branches: Setting: Where? When? / Thoughts? / Events: Who was involved? Why? / Conversations? / Entertaining parts? / Descriptive details?

   b Write your opening sentence. Make it as engaging as possible. If it doesn't sound great, don't worry. Go back to it later.

   c Write about one side of A4 in total. Remember to use effective verbs and adjectives. Perhaps include some humour and imagery such as metaphors.

Taking it further

Explore some more creative non-fiction. Read *Chinese Cinderella* or *Falling Leaves* by Adeline Yen Mah.

How did I do?

	✔
I know that creative non-fiction accounts are true stories that employ narrative or poetic devices to entertain readers.	☐
I know that creative non-fiction is about a true event, but includes dialogue, thoughts, descriptive detail and carefully selected vocabulary.	☐

Teacher's tips

When you write your autobiographical account, have a *thesaurus* to hand to help you diversify your vocabulary.

32: How? What? Why?

In this unit you will explore:
- how to write an instruction manual
- how to write an explanatory article.

Get started

An instruction manual guides people in how to do something. It is organised and easy to follow.

An explanatory article uses both words and images to give details about a particular topic.

Practice

1. Which of the following do you think are needed in a manual and which are more likely be found in an explanatory article?
   - step-by-step instructions
   - clear language
   - details
   - history
   - technical jargon
   - facts and figures
   - reasons

Challenge

Instruction manual

Read this extract taken from a DIY instruction manual.

> **How to fix a leaking tap**
>
> There are two kinds of tap mechanism: Washer and Ceramic disc.
>
> **Washer taps** are available in a wide variety of styles but they all work in the same way. Turning the handle closes a washer against the water inlet inside the tap, shutting off the supply. With reverse pressure taps ('Supataps') you can fix a leaking washer without having to turn the water off. However, it is always preferable to turn off the water supply before you start.
>
> **Ceramic disc taps** have revolving discs instead of washers. They usually go from off to fully on in a quarter turn, making them convenient for elderly or disabled people. Wear is less of a problem than with washer taps, but if there is a problem you have to replace a disc cartridge, which is more expensive than fitting a washer.

2. Outline what the writer does in the first line of this extract.

3. In terms of subject, how does the writer divide his paragraphs?

4. Outline what the writer does in the first line of his two main paragraphs.

5. Look at the extract as a whole. Identify the sentences where the main instructions appear.

6 You are going to write a set of instructions for how to take a picture with a digital camera or mobile phone camera and download it onto a computer to print. Look back at the extract from a manual shown opposite. Use this structure and layout to help you.

  a Make a note of each step that you make when taking and downloading images.
  b Make sure that the steps are in the correct order so that someone else can follow them easily. Make sure that your language is clear.
  c Test that your instructions work and can be followed.
  d Provide some images to help the readers.

Explanatory article

When dinosaurs first appeared about 230 million years ago the world was very different. There were very few of the animal groups we recognise today – no mammals, no birds and no lizards.

What? No grass?
The difference was also apparent in the plant kingdom. Plant life would have seemed very drab. There were no flowering plants, so nothing like most of the common trees and shrubs today. There was no grass. Instead, low ground cover would have been ferns and mosses.

A giant desert
The continents of the Triassic Earth were configured differently to today. All the land masses on the planet were joined together into one huge continent called Pangaea. This stretched from pole to pole and its central region was a vast inhospitable desert.

New life
The Late Triassic was an innovative time in the animal kingdom. By the end of the period not only the dinosaurs had appeared but also pterosaurs (flying reptiles), various kinds of marine reptiles, the first crocodiles and turtles, and the earliest true mammals. Towards the end of the Triassic, 220 million years ago, there was another extinction, which wiped out many of the non-dinosaurs.

7 Look at the way the information is divided. Make a note of subheadings.

8 Explanatory writing relies a lot on nouns. From the text, make a list of common, proper and abstract nouns (at least two of each).

9 There are some specialist terms in this article. List a few of these words.

10 List any facts or figures in the article.

11 Whom do you think this article is aimed at and why?

How did I do?

✔ I know that an instruction manual is a clear set of instructions about how to do something.

☐ I know that an explanatory article is made up of text and images.

☐ I know that an explanatory article tells people about a topic and usually answers the questions what, how and why.

Taking it further

Select a topic that you know well or have studied in school and decide on an audience that you will write for. Write an explanatory article for a website about your topic. Use a combination of words and images. Also, divide your article using subheadings. You might even provide links to explain jargon or for further reading.

Teacher's tips

Once you have written your instructions for how to take pictures with a digital camera and download the images, why not test whether your instructions are clear by giving them to a friend to follow? This will tell you whether you have succeeded!

33: A balancing act

In this unit you will explore:
- how to write a balanced analysis of a topic.

Get started

A balanced analysis of a topic considers both sides and is written in an impartial and unbiased way.

Practice

1 Look at the following biased sentences. Identify which words make them sound biased.

    a Having to pay for a television licence is ludicrous.
    b The M25 is a nightmare road.
    c Public transport in the UK is a joke.
    d Capital punishment is inhumane.

2 Rewrite the sentences so that they sound unbiased.

Challenge

People have different opinions about whether or not computers are a good thing.

3 What reasons might people have for thinking computers are good?

4 What reasons might people have for thinking they aren't good?

Read the two extracts printed below. They are sections taken from two students' essays on the pros and cons of computers.

a Computers are good because they allow us to do things we wouldn't be able to do without them. They can calculate very difficult sums and carry out complicated tasks which we cannot. They are bad though because people lose jobs and computers aren't reliable as they crash.

b Some people believe that computers are a blessing: they allow us to carry out difficult and long calculations which we would otherwise have been unable to do. Calculating the answer to two million three hundred and seventy six multiplied by thirty seven thousand is no longer a problem now that we have computers to hand. However, computers are machines and as such they are prone to faults and problems. Sometimes they become infected with viruses. There are thousands of them out there. That's why McAfee software was invented, and sometimes computers crash. Another point raised against computers is the fact that they are starting to replace people. You don't have to stand in a queue to buy a train ticket from a person any more. You can buy one from a machine now. On the plus side companies are saving money but on the minus side people are losing their jobs.

5 The points that the two students make are similar. What are these points?

6 Extract **b** is better in terms of style. What words does the second student use to link her sentences together so that she moves from one point to another easily?

7 What else does the second student do that makes her writing better?

8 Match the words below with the function they carry out in an essay.

Words	Functions
Some people believe However Others think that On the other hand Similarly Likewise Whilst Whereas	Raising opponents' views Suggesting a contrast Suggesting a comparison, similarity

9 Make a list of points for and against school uniform.

10 Now, write an essay about school uniforms analysing the two sides. Remember to structure your essay by writing an introduction, main body and conclusion (see Unit 14).

You might start:

> School uniform is a much debated topic. Some people believe that it provides a school with an easily recognisable identity, that it gets students in the right frame of mind for work and that it helps to prevent bullying. Others feel it is an outdated system that stunts individuality and prevents students from feeling relaxed and performing at their best.

Taking it further

Write an essay analysing the ways that modern life in Britain is both better and worse than it was 200 years ago. Remember to look at both sides of the topic, including both positive and negative things about life today. Also, provide specific examples to give your essay more weight.

How did I do?

- ✓ I know that analysing a topic in a balanced way means writing about both sides of a debate.
- ☐ I know that impartial language and examples should be used.

Teacher's tips

If you have difficulty coming up with points both for and against school uniform, talk to a friend about the subject. See what they think. This may help you.

34: Synthesising information

In this unit you will explore:
- what synthesising information means
- synthesising information from different sources.

Get started

Synthesising information means drawing information together from two or more sources for a particular purpose, and avoiding contradiction and repetition.

Practice

On a small scale it is possible to synthesise information in sentences. Here is an example:

Luke is aged 15. Luke's favourite sport is football. Luke is playing for the under-16s this Saturday.

This becomes:
Fifteen-year-old Luke, whose favourite sport is football, is playing for the under-16s this Saturday.

1 Do the same with the following sentences.

    a Jane Austen was a writer. Jane Austen lived in the nineteenth century. Jane Austen wrote *Emma*.
    b Cats get fleas. Fleas are an irritation to cats. Cats benefit from occasional applications of flea powder.
    c Stephen Hawking wrote *A Brief History of Time*. *A Brief History of Time* is an influential work. Stephen Hawking is a leading figure in modern physics.

Challenge

2 Read the pieces of information below and make notes on the main points. Bear in mind how reliable each source is.

3 Synthesise the information into an entry on Ronald Morgan for the book *Who's Who in Crime?*

St Cuthbert's School report, autumn term 1977

Ronald has made a good start at St Cuthbert's, showing an imaginative approach to English, a talent for mathematical calculation, and a single-minded determination. However, he should try to mix more with other boys.

The *Shorehampton Echo*, 5 June 1989

The Shorehampton branch of Floyd's Bank has been the target of a £500,000 raid. Staff arrived this morning to find a body-sized hole in the floor, surrounded by rubble. They then discovered that the money was missing.

Police believe the crime to be the work of one man, whom they have already dubbed 'The Mole'. A thin junior officer was dispatched into the narrow tunnel with a torch and emerged in the overgrown garden of a derelict house across the street.

'He must have been digging for several months,' said Inspector Doug Understreet. 'We're looking for a man seen entering the abandoned house. He is of slight build, may have a Welsh accent, and has muddy trousers.'

The Man they called the Mole: A Life of Ronnie Morgan

Born into a humble Cardiff terrace in 1966, Ronald Morgan was a quiet boy who won a scholarship to an elite private school. However, he failed to fulfil early promise. An only child, Ronald was coddled by his mother but found his father a cold and distant figure. Perhaps Ronald was doomed to turn to crime . . .

BBC News report, 14 July 2012

We have breaking news that a man run over by a bus in Piccadilly is the arch-criminal Ronald Morgan. The bus driver reported that a hole suddenly appeared in the road a few feet from Bungay's Bank, and a man's head appeared. The driver had no time to stop.

Daily Sportsman, 14 July 2012

Mole's Fatal Miscalculation

Oops! A criminal miscalculation finally caught up with Ronnie the Mole today. Bank job Number 21 turned out to be his last . . .

Trisha magazine

The Ronnie the World Never Knew – by the woman who loved him

The world knows my Ronnie as a heartless criminal who lived a champagne lifestyle on the proceeds of nineteen bank robberies. But I knew him as a sensitive man who loved hamsters and gave me a diamond ring the size of the Ritz . . .

Letter, 10 July 2012

Dear Mum,

Your loving Ronald here. Obviously I cannot reveal my whereabouts, but I want you to know that I'm all right. The coppers say they're on to me, but no way. If only Dad was alive to see that I've made something of myself. I have one last job planned, then I'm retiring. Don't worry.

Love, Ronnie

Taking it further

Make notes on a public figure, using a number of sources. Then write a short biographical feature.

Apply the same approach to a current news topic.

How did I do?

✓

- I know that synthesising information means selecting from several sources and combining what is found into a single account.
- I know that it is important to be selective and ensure that there is no repetition or contradiction.

Teacher's tips

Synthesising information is a skill that comes with practice. Aim to use as few words as possible when you combine the information you read. Use a highlighter to identify key points which you will draw together later.

35: Comparing texts – ideas

In this unit you will explore:
- comparing ideas in non-fiction texts
- how ideas are presented in non-fiction.

Get started

You need to be able to compare contrasting ideas on a subject in different texts. This requires you to grasp the most important points in each text and to see how the ideas are similar and how they are different.

Practice

1. Compare the following pairs of sentences. How are the ideas they contain different?

a.i Education is the key to success.	**a.ii** Learning is always worthwhile.
b.i Money is unimportant.	**b.ii** Money can't buy happiness.
c.i Animals matter more than people.	**c.ii** Animals have rights.
d.i Meat is murder!	**d.ii** Vegetarianism is better for you.
e.i Yesterday's terrorists are today's freedom fighters.	**e.ii** Society admires those who resist oppression.

Challenge

Read the letters below. They have been written to the 'Have your say' page of a newspaper.

a Young people today have a more difficult time than in any previous era. They have to go to school, and there is a lot of pressure for them to succeed there. Schools are large and impersonal, and teachers are overstretched, so that individual differences are not catered for and bullying is often overlooked.

There is also a culture of underachievement – it is not 'cool' to be seen to do well, especially for boys. So pupils are pulled in different directions. Some would like to learn more but are prevented from doing so by other pupils who scorn academic achievement because they are not capable of it themselves. Some are caught between peer pressure and parental pressure. On the other hand, some parents themselves have mixed feelings about their children's success.

Youngsters are growing up in a rapidly changing and confusing world. Wars and the threat of environmental disaster are causes for anxiety. Big business, meanwhile, encourages youngsters to care more about their trainers or PlayStation. No wonder they are confused or appear to be indifferent.

b Kids today have got it made – or so it seems. They have more leisure than ever before, and have the chance to get a decent education instead of going out to work at the age of twelve. They also have more money to spend than ever before, and more products to spend it on. True, schools are not perfect, but a bit of rough and tumble never hurt anyone. Quite the opposite, in fact. We hear a lot of talk about bullying, but, frankly, the victims need to learn to stick up for themselves.

All pupils are capable of doing well at school, but not all make the most of their educational opportunities. Many are all too easily led astray, opting for classroom popularity rather than hard work. One possible solution here may be to bring back single-sex schools, as girls work better in them, and boys in a boys' school will not be trying to impress their female classmates.

The world faces big problems – international conflicts and environmental threats – so we need our youngsters to pull themselves together and get ready to sort them out. The future lies with them!

2 Make a list of the main points in each letter.

3 Now compare the two letters. Make a table of points on which they agree and the points on which they disagree.

4 Compare the tone of the two letters. Which, overall, is more sympathetic towards young people? Which is more casual in tone?

Taking it further

- Visit the websites of political parties and see what views and policies they present. For example, what do they say about education, or crime? On what points do they agree, or disagree?
- Write a questionnaire to compare people's views on education. For example, is it to prepare people for work, or to bring out the best in them? Try your questionnaire on several people and compare their views.

How did I do?

I know that to compare two sets of ideas it is necessary to understand the main points in each text. ✓

I know that the next step is to see on what points the opinions are the same, and on what points they differ.

Teacher's tips

Sometimes differences are expressed in subtle ways. The **connotations** of words are important. For example, the same person might be described as *easy-going* or *lazy*. The first description has positive connotations but the second has negative suggestions.

36: Comparing texts – values

In this unit you will explore:
- what values there are in literature
- how to spot values in literature.

Get started

Writers often include their own values – their deeply held beliefs about what is right and important in life – in their work. Even single words can contain values. These values are partly personal to the writer, but they can also reflect the attitudes of society, so they can change over time.

Practice

1. Some words mean different things to different people. What do you understand by the following words?

   a courage
   b freedom
   c honour
   d heroism
   e glory

Challenge

Read this extract from Alfred Lord Tennyson's poem, 'The Charge of the Light Brigade'.

> 'Forward, the Light Brigade!'
> Was there a man dismayed?
> Not tho' the soldier knew
>   Someone had blundered:
> Theirs not to make reply,
> Theirs not to reason why,
> Theirs but to do and die:
> Into the valley of Death
> Rode the six hundred. . . .
> Cannon to right of them,
> Cannon to left of them,
> Cannon behind them
> Volley'd and thundered;
>
> Stormed at with shot and shell,
> While horse and hero fell,
> They that had fought so well
> Came through the jaws of Death,
> Back from the mouth of hell,
> All that was left of them,
> Left of six hundred.
>
> When can their glory fade?
> O the wild charge they made!
> All the world wondered.
> Honour the charge they made!
> Honour the Light Brigade,
> Noble six hundred!

2. What does the poem suggest a soldier's attitude towards war should be? What words indicate this?

3. What does it suggest people should think of soldiers who risk death or die in battle? Again, what words indicate this?

Now read the following extract from 'Dulce et Decorum est', a poem by First World War poet Wilfred Owen about a poison gas attack in the trenches. The title comes from the Latin poet Horace, who wrote *Dulce et decorum est pro patria mori*: 'It is sweet and right to die for your country.'

> Gas! Gas! Quick, boys! – An ecstasy of fumbling,
> Fitting the clumsy helmets just in time;
> But someone still was yelling out and stumbling,
> And flound'ring like a man in fire or lime . . .
> Dim, through the misty panes and thick green light,
> As under a green sea, I saw him drowning.
> In all my dreams, before my helpless sight,
> He plunges at me, guttering, choking, drowning.
>
> If in some smothering dreams you too could pace
> Behind the wagon that we flung him in,
> And watch the white eyes writhing in his face,
> His hanging face, like a devil's sick of sin;
> If you could hear, at every jolt, the blood
> Come gargling from the froth-corrupted lungs,
> Obscene as cancer, bitter as the cud
> Of vile, incurable sores on innocent tongues,
> My friend, you would not tell with such high zest
> To children ardent for some desperate glory,
> The old Lie; Dulce et Decorum est
> Pro patria mori.

4 Compare Wilfred Owen's view of war with that of Tennyson.

5 What words in this poem make war seem lacking in glory?

6 What is Owen's attitude towards the 'glory' of war?

7 How do Owen's views on war compare with your own?

8 How do you think attitudes have changed between 1870, the date of Tennyson's poem, and 1918, when Owen's was completed?

Taking it further

- Read 'Who's for the game?' by Jessie Pope (available online). Owen wrote 'Dulce et Decorum est' to her because he felt her poems lacked insight into what war was really like. He addresses her in the second verse quoted here.
- Read Siegfried Sassoon's poem 'Suicide in the Trenches' (also online) and compare its values with those of Tennyson and Owen.
- Write about your own views of war.

How did I do?

	✓
I know that writing often contains values – deeply held beliefs about what is right and important.	☐
I know that literature often embodies values – both personal and social.	☐

Teacher's tips

To answer question 5, look at how Wilfred Owen describes the soldier who doesn't get his gas mask on in time, in verse 1 and verse 2.

37: Comparing texts – emotions

In this unit you will explore:
- how literature conveys emotions
- how to compare emotions in literature.

Get started

Both fiction and non-fiction can contain emotions, such as anger, sadness, regret, fear and happiness. Writers often want to convey their emotions to us. They may do so in different ways.

Practice

Because emotions matter a lot to us, there are many words for emotions, some of which are similar but not quite the same.

1 Consider the following pairs.

irritation – anger	regret – misery
fury – resentment	happiness – jubilation
sadness – grief	enthusiasm – elation

Now look the words up in the dictionary to check the 'official' meanings.

Challenge

Read this speech by a Native American chief, Inmutooyahlatlat (Chief Joseph), and answer the questions that follow.

> I do not understand why nothing is done for my people. I have heard talk and talk, and nothing is done. Good words do not last long unless they amount to something. Words do not pay for my dead people. They do not pay for my country, now overrun by white men. They do not protect my father's grave. They do not pay for all my horses and cattle. Good words will not give me back my children. Good words will not give my people good health and stop them from dying. Good words will not get my people a home where they can live in peace and take care of themselves. I am tired of talk that comes to nothing. It makes my heart sick when I remember all the good words and all the broken promises.

2 What feelings does Chief Joseph have about his people?

3 What does he feel about white men?

4 How does the repetition of 'talk' and 'Good words' help to express his emotions?

5 Overall, what different emotions is Chief Joseph expressing?

6 How effective do you think Chief Joseph's speech is? For example, would it be more expressive if he went into more detail about what the white men had done, or if he used vivid adjectives to say how badly they had behaved?

Now read this speech, from Shakespeare's *As You Like It*, in which a young noble, Orlando, complains about how his older brother, Oliver, has treated him since their father's death.

> His horses are bred better; for, besides that they are fair with their feeding, they are taught their manage, and to that end riders dearly hired: but I, his brother, gain nothing under him but growth; for the which his animals on his dunghills are as much bound to him as I. Besides this nothing that he so plentifully gives me, the something that nature gave me his countenance seems to take from me: he lets me feed with his hinds [deer], bars me the place of a brother, and, as much as in him lies, mines my gentility with my education. This is it, Adam, that grieves me; and the spirit of my father, which I think is within me, begins to mutiny against this servitude: I will no longer endure it, though yet I know no wise remedy how to avoid it.

7 What is the emotional effect of Orlando comparing himself with his brother's horses and the animals on his brother's dunghills (piles of rubbish and manure)?

8 How does he feel about not getting an education fit for his nobility?

9 What emotion does Orlando express near the end of the passage?

10 Compare the following.

   a the situations of Chief Joseph and Orlando
   b the emotions they express
   c how they express their emotions

11 Compare the passages above and opposite with that of

   a Shylock in *The Merchant of Venice* (Act 3, scene 1, 'Hath not a Jew eyes . . .') and
   b Caliban in *The Tempest* (Act 1, scene 2, 'This island's mine . . .').

12 Compare Chief Joseph's repetition of 'Good words' with Mark Antony's repeated description of Brutus as honourable in his speech beginning 'Friends, Romans, countrymen . . .' (*Julius Caesar*, Act 3, scene 2).

How did I do?

	✓
I know that writing often expresses emotions such as anger, sadness or fear.	☐
I know that emotions are subtle.	☐
I know that a writer may express a mixture of different emotions, and do so in a variety of ways.	☐

Teacher's tips

If you find the extract from *As You Like It* difficult to understand, you may find the following website helpful: nfs.sparknotes.com/asyoulikeit. Look at Act 1 Scene 1 where you will find a modern version of the script next to the original.

38: Comparing modern and older texts

In this unit you will explore:
- dialogue in modern and older texts
- characterisation
- style.

Get started

Older texts differ from modern ones in several ways. They are more formal, characters are often portrayed less *naturalistically*, and you may be unfamiliar with some of the language used. However, both modern and older texts deal with similar themes and emotions.

Practice

Language changes with time, as people gradually use words differently. One way in which English changes is by new words coming into it from other languages.

1 Use a dictionary, either in book form or online, that gives word derivations (origins) to find out which languages the following words originally came from.

   a algebra
   b assassin
   c bungalow
   d juggernaut
   e ski
   f toboggan

Challenge

Read Extract **a**, in which a woman has snagged her dress on a soldier's spur in passing, at night. Then answer the questions that follow.

a He looked hard into her eyes when she raised them for a moment; Bathsheba looked down again, for his gaze was too strong to be received point-blank with her own. But she had obliquely noticed that he was young and slim, and that he wore three chevrons upon his sleeve.
   Bathsheba pulled again.
   'You are a prisoner, miss; it is no use blinking the matter,' said the soldier, drily. 'I must cut your dress if you are in such a hurry.'
   'Yes – please do!' she exclaimed, helplessly.
   'It wouldn't be necessary if you could wait a moment,' and he unwound a cord from the little wheel. She withdrew her own hand, but, whether by accident or design, he touched it. Bathsheba was vexed; she hardly knew why.
   His unravelling went on, but it nevertheless seemed coming to no end. She looked at him again.
   'Thank you for the sight of such a beautiful face!' said the young sergeant, without ceremony.
   She coloured with embarrassment. ''Twas unwillingly shown,' she replied, stiffly, and with as much dignity – which was very little – as she could infuse into a position of captivity.

(Thomas Hardy, *Far From the Madding Crowd*, 1874)

2 What, to a modern reader, seems old-fashioned about the way in which the characters relate to each other?

3 What phrases in the passage seem formal?

4 What does the final sentence mean and what makes it sound like an older text?

Now read Extract **b** and answer the questions that follow.

> **b** I must have been on to my third lobotomiser when the boy I'd noticed before turned and looked at me. He was just another Chippy guy in a beat up leather jacket and wild, greasy-looking hair, but he turned round and our eyes met and that was it.
>
> I guess sometimes there are moments when people's lives change and they don't even know it. They can look back later, when everything's different, and say yes, that was the start of it – that's when it all began, and I didn't even notice.
>
> Well, I noticed all right, and it was like – I can't explain. It was like everything shattering apart, y'know? I mean everything. Things I thought I knew. Stuff I'd been taught. The foundation of my life is what I'm talking about here, and I felt it shift, and if you've never felt that then you don't know what I'm talking about. Anyway, it shifted that night and shattered apart and Ma and Pa Askew never got their sweet little Zoe back. Oh, they thought they still had her, but they didn't. It was somebody else.
>
> Somebody else entirely.
>
> (Robert Swindells, *Daz 4 Zoe*, 1995)

5 Modern texts are often informal, use colloquial phrases and slang, and address the reader in a conversational tone. Find examples of this sort of language in Extract **b**.

6 What is modern about the phrase 'their sweet little Zoe'? (Is that how she sees herself?)

7 Why does the final line of Extract **b** sound modern?

Taking it further

- Read the previous chapter of *Daz 4 Zoe* (Chapter 8, page 20 in the 1995 edition). It is written through the eyes of the boy Zoe talks about here.
- Compare both accounts of a first meeting with Romeo and Juliet's meeting, in Shakespeare's *Romeo and Juliet* (Act 1, scene 5, from 'What lady is that, which doth enrich the hand / Of yonder knight?').

How did I do?

	✓
I know that language has changed since older texts were written, even though they are mostly concerned with the same issues as modern texts.	☐
I know that modern texts tend to be less formal in tone, and to experiment with language, often breaking the rules of grammar.	☐

Teacher's tips

To complete question 1, why not go to *Oxford English Dictionaries Online* at http://oxforddictionaries.com, which includes the origins of words. For question 7, think about whether the last line is a complete sentence.

39: Dramatic impact

In this unit you will explore:
- how drama catches our attention
- how action and language work together
- the importance of tension, conflict and resolution.

Get started

Drama depends on tension and conflict. It must arouse our interest, create tension somehow, make us want to know how the tension will be resolved, and then resolve it in a way which we, the audience, find satisfying.

Practice

One way in which you can make a sentence sound more direct and forceful is to use the *active voice* and avoid the *passive voice*.

Example: *A car ran him over* (active). *He was run over by a car* (passive).

There is nothing wrong with the passive voice, but it has a different effect from the active voice.

1 Change the following passive sentences to active ones and suggest how the two versions differ in meaning and tone.

   a The boys were overtaken by the girls.
   b Your dinner has been eaten by the dog.
   c I was given a helping hand.
   d 'Mistakes have been made,' said a government spokesman.
   e He was led astray by older boys.

Challenge

The extract below is set in a comprehensive school. A new teacher, Mr Wright, has had to move his lesson to the staffroom. To teach his class about prejudice, he has announced that brown-eyed people are superior to blue-eyed. This has split the class into two groups.

Read the extract and answer the questions that follow.

4TH BOY: . . . Come on, let's get them, shall we? (*More agreement, but no advance. Some brown eyes are still nervous. The* 4TH BOY *and the* 3RD BOY *mumble to each other again, slowly move over to the* LONER, *who is leaning against the pigeon holes with his paperback. The other brown eyes latch on, move across behind him. The* LONER, *unaware for some seconds, looks up, stares around, backs away into the pigeon holes*) Blue eye!

3RD BOY: Bum.

1ST BLACK KID: Scum.

2ND BLACK KID: Trash.

4TH BOY: Pig.

LONER: Wha'? Don't be daft. (*to* 3RD BOY) I'm your mate.

3RD BOY: Not any longer, y'not. (*They are still only half serious*)

4TH BOY (*poking the* LONER): 'Cos you're inferior. Ron says so, an' he's our leader. But you're our slave, blue eye. You have t'do anythin' we tell y'.

LONER: Get lost.

4TH BOY (*still poking him*): Don't insult y'betters, Jimbo. Y'might not live t'tell the tale.

LONER: Leave me alone.

4TH BOY (*lifting up his foot*): My shoelace is undone. Tie it for me, blue eye.

LONER: Tie it y'self.

4TH BOY (*slaps him across the face. No force*): You do it, slave.
(*Giggles and laughter from the brown eyes. The blue eyes are moved together by the* 1ST BOY)

1ST BOY: Take no notice. Jimmy. (*The blue eyes huddle together. We see that the* 1ST BOY *is directing them*)

4TH BOY: Tie my shoelace, blue eye.

LONER: Won't.

4TH BOY (*snatches the book off him, passes it back to the* 3RD BOY, *who throws it aimlessly over his shoulder*): I said *tie it*. (*He takes hold of his head, pushes it downwards. The* LONER *struggles.*)

MR WRIGHT: Now, one thing I won't tolerate is physical violence, I should have . . .

(Alan Bleasdale, *No More Sitting on the Old School Bench*)

2 How does tension develop during the passage? (Don't forget the action, shown in the stage directions.)

3 How does the action revealed in the first stage direction engage our attention?

4 Who do you sympathise with in this extract?

5 Who appears to have most power?

6 How do you think the tension between the 4th boy and the Loner will be resolved?

7 How might you expect this scene to develop?

8 What is your view of Mr Wright's teaching methods?

Taking it further

- What tensions in your own school do you think could be turned into the subject of a play with dramatic impact?
- Analyse the sources of tension in a TV soap episode.

How did I do?

I know that drama is based on the resolution of tension. ✓

I know that words and action work together to engage our interest and make a dramatic impact.

Teacher's tips

Remember, the **active** voice involves someone doing something, and the **passive** voice involves something being done to someone. When you answer question 6 and question 8, bear in mind there is no right answer.

40: Shakespeare's world – the context

In this unit you will explore:
- how Shakespeare's world differed from ours
- how this is reflected in Shakespeare's plays.

Get started

Shakespeare's world was different from ours in many ways.

- Class differences were extreme and hard to escape.
- People believed that kings and queens were appointed by God.
- Everyone believed in God and went to church; most people believed in magic; many believed in astrology.
- Women had little power and no career opportunities. They were expected to obey their fathers, then, when married, their husbands.
- Technology and medicine were undeveloped; life was physically hard and disease was common.

Practice

1 How do the images below reflect Shakespeare's world?

a Out, out, brief candle!
   Life's but a walking shadow, a poor player
   That struts and frets his hour upon the stage

(Macbeth, talking about life, in *Macbeth*, Act 5, scene 5)

b Have I not heard the sea puff'd up with winds
   Rage like an angry boar chafed with sweat?

(Petruchio in *The Taming of the Shrew*, Act 1, scene 2)

c In one little body
   Thou counterfeit'st a bark*, a sea, a wind;   *ship
   For still thy eyes, which I may call the sea,
   Do ebb and flow with tears; the bark thy body is,
   Sailing in this salt flood.

(Capulet in *Romeo and Juliet*, Act 3, scene 5)

Challenge

Read the following passage from *Romeo and Juliet*. It comes just after the one above. Juliet's father has just heard that Juliet will not agree to the marriage he has arranged for her.

Juliet: Good father, I beseech you on my knees,
Hear me with patience but to speak a word.

Capulet: Hang thee, young baggage! disobedient wretch!
I tell thee what: get thee to church o' Thursday,
Or never after look me in the face:
Speak not, reply not, do not answer me;
My fingers itch. Wife, we scarce thought us blest
That God had lent us but this only child;
But now I see this one is one too much,
And that we have a curse in having her:
Out on her, hilding*!

*worthless creature

(*Romeo and Juliet*, Act 3, scene 5)

2 How does Juliet's tone reflect Shakespeare's world?

3 How does her father's response reflect it?

4 What does the speech reveal about the Elizabethan attitude to God?

5 Now read the passages that follow. In the first, Cassius suggests that Brutus is as good a man as Caesar. In the second, Calpurnia tries to persuade her husband, Caesar, to stay at home that day. Comment on what the passages tell us about Shakespeare's world. In particular, what question, hotly debated at the time, is he exploring here?

How did I do?

I know that Shakespeare's world differed from ours in terms of class system, beliefs, medicine, technology and attitudes to gender. ✓ ☐

I know that these differences reveal themselves in Shakespeare's plays. ☐

a Cassius: Men at some time are masters of their fates:
The fault, dear Brutus, is not in our stars,
But in ourselves, that we are underlings.

(*Julius Caesar*, Act 1, scene 2)

b Calpurnia: A lioness hath whelped* in the streets;
And graves have yawn'd, and yielded up their dead;
Fierce fiery warriors fought upon the clouds,
In ranks and squadrons and right form of war,
Which drizzled blood upon the Capitol;
The noise of battle hurtled in the air,
Horses did neigh, and dying men did groan,
And ghosts did shriek and squeal about the streets.
O Caesar! these things are beyond all use*,
And I do fear them.

*given birth

*have never happened before

Caesar: What can be avoided
Whose end is purposed by the mighty gods?
Yet Caesar shall go forth; for these predictions
Are to the world in general as to Caesar.

(*Julius Caesar*, Act 1, scene 2)

Teacher's tips

Sometimes, reading over Shakespeare's words a few times helps you to get to the meaning. If you still have difficulty understanding these extracts, you can always look online at nfs.sparknotes.com.

41: Shakespeare's language

In this unit you will explore:
- how Shakespeare's language differs from modern English
- Shakespeare's inventiveness with language
- blank verse and prose.

Get started

Shakespeare invented many words and phrases. He used imagery, rhythm and sound effects (such as alliteration) very expressively. He also wrote in a way that would appeal both to uneducated commoners and to nobles.

When reading Shakespeare, read to the end of each sentence, not the end of the line, and try to understand the overall sense.

Practice

1. These phrases were all invented or popularised by Shakespeare. What do they mean?

   a A fool's paradise
   b It's vanished into thin air
   c It's all Greek to me
   d He won't budge an inch
   e Make a virtue of necessity
   f Don't stand on ceremony
   g No rhyme or reason
   h What the dickens!

Challenge

Shakespeare often got his stories or information from other sources. Read the following to see how he transformed Lord North's translation of the Latin poet Plutarch's description of Cleopatra, Queen of Egypt.

North's Plutarch	Shakespeare
. . . she disdained to set forward otherwise, but to take her barge in the river of Cydnus, the poop whereof was of gold, the sails of purple, and the oars of silver, which kept stroke in rowing after the sound of the music of flutes, hautboys, citherns, viols, and such other instruments as they played upon in the barge. And now for the person of herself: she was laid under a pavilion of cloth of gold of tissue, apparelled and attired like the goddess Venus, commonly drawn in picture: and hard by her, on either hand of her, pretty fair boys apparelled as painters do set forth god Cupid, with little fans in their hands, with the which they fanned wind upon her.	The barge she sat in, like a burnish'd throne, Burn'd on the water: the poop* was beaten gold; Purple the sails, and so perfumed that The winds were love-sick with them; the oars were silver, Which to the tune of flutes kept stroke, and made The water which they beat to follow faster, As amorous** of their strokes. For her own person, It beggar'd all description: she did lie In her pavilion – cloth-of-gold of tissue – O'er-picturing that Venus where we see The fancy outwork*** nature: on each side her Stood pretty dimpled boys, like smiling Cupids, With divers-colour'd fans, whose wind did seem To glow the delicate cheeks which they did cool, And what they undid did. . . . *poop – rear part of the barge **amorous – loving ***fancy outwork – imagination outdo (*Antony and Cleopatra*, Act 2, scene 2)

2 Compare the two descriptions of the sails.

   a What word does Shakespeare's description start with, and why?
   b How does Shakespeare use alliteration (repetition of a sound)?
   c What fanciful image does Shakespeare use?

3 What image does Shakespeare use to describe the water around the oars?

4 Cleopatra is fanned by 'pretty boys' in both descriptions. How is Shakespeare's description here more poetic than North's?

5 Overall, what does Shakespeare's version add to North's description?

6 Shakespeare could also write speeches that were simple but stirring. Read the following, which is part of Henry V's speech to his army before a battle on St Crispin's Day. How is it different from the description of Cleopatra, and how does it fit its purpose?

> This story shall the good man teach his son;
> And Crispin Crispian shall ne'er go by,
> From this day to the ending of the world,
> But we in it shall be remember'd;
> We few, we happy few, we band of brothers;
> For he today that sheds his blood with me
> Shall be my brother; be he ne'er so vile*,   *common
> This day shall gentle his condition*:   *make him a gentleman
> And gentlemen in England now a-bed
> Shall think themselves accursed they were not here,
> And hold their manhoods cheap whiles any speaks
> That fought with us upon Saint Crispin's day.
>
> (*Henry V*, Act 4, scene 3)

7 Shakespeare's nobles speak in *blank verse*, as in Henry V's speech. His commoners usually speak in prose. A typical line of blank (unrhymed) verse has five pairs of syllables, as in Henry's first line.

Read the speeches in this unit aloud to see how Shakespeare varies this slightly to match the sense.

For example, the second line in the description of Cleopatra has an extra syllable. Does this speed the line up or slow it down?

In Henry's speech, the fifth line has an extra syllable. What is the effect here?

How did I do?

☑

☐ I know that Shakespeare's vocabulary is in some ways different from ours.

☐ I know that Shakespeare was exceptionally gifted in his choice of words, his imagery and his use of rhythm to match meaning.

Teacher's tips

If you find answering question 1 tricky, it may help you to ask a friend or to do an internet search. **Blank verse** means unrhymed lines written in *iambic pentameter,* which is a set rhythm that sounds like this: *di dum di dum di dum di dum di dum.*

42: Tragedy, comedy, history

In this unit you will explore:
- the different types of play that Shakespeare wrote
- what their typical features are.

Get started

Shakespeare's plays can be divided into three main types.

- Tragedies – involve conflict, revenge and deaths, including that of a tragic hero (sometimes a heroine too), who makes a fatal mistake.
- Comedies – include misunderstandings (eventually sorted out), humour (including puns), disguise, love, marriage and a happy ending.
- Histories – based on real events (including battles), focusing on kingship, loyalty and patriotism, ending in peace.

Practice

1 From what you know about the different types of Shakespearean play, what type of play do the following lines come from?

a Once more unto the breach, dear friends, once more;
Or close the wall up with our English dead.

b Why should a dog, a horse, a rat, have life,
And thou no breath at all? Thou'lt come no more,
Never, never, never, never, never!

c If you will then see the fruits of the sport, mark his first approach before my lady: he will come to her in yellow stockings, and 'tis a colour she abhors, and cross-gartered, a fashion she detests.

Challenge

2 What type of play do Extracts **a** and **b** below come from? Make notes on what features helped you to decide.

a

Queen Gertrude: No, no, the drink, the drink,– O my dear Hamlet,–
The drink, the drink! I am poison'd. (*Dies*)

Hamlet: O villainy! Ho! let the door be lock'd:
Treachery! Seek it out.

Laertes: It is here, Hamlet: Hamlet, thou art slain;
No medicine in the world can do thee good;
In thee there is not half an hour of life;
The treacherous instrument is in thy hand,
Unbated and envenom'd: the foul practice
Hath turn'd itself on me lo, here I lie,
Never to rise again: thy mother's poison'd:
I can no more: the king, the king's to blame.

Hamlet:	The point! – envenom'd too! Then, venom, to thy work. (*Stabs KING CLAUDIUS*)
All:	Treason! treason!
King Claudius:	O, yet defend me, friends; I am but hurt.
Hamlet:	Here, thou incestuous, murderous, damned Dane, Drink off this potion. Is thy union here? Follow my mother. (*KING CLAUDIUS dies*)
Laertes:	He is justly served; It is a poison temper'd by himself. Exchange forgiveness with me, noble Hamlet: Mine and my father's death come not upon thee, Nor thine on me. (*Dies*)

b

Sir Toby Belch:	What wilt thou do?
Maria:	I will drop in his way some obscure epistles of love; wherein, by the colour of his beard, the shape of his leg, the manner of his gait, the expressure of his eye, forehead, and complexion, he shall find himself most feelingly personated. I can write very like my lady your niece: on a forgotten matter we can hardly make distinction of our hands.
Sir Toby Belch:	Excellent! I smell a device.
Sir Andrew:	I have't in my nose too.
Sir Toby Belch:	He shall think, by the letters that thou wilt drop, that they come from my niece, and that she's in love with him.
Maria:	My purpose is, indeed, a horse of that colour.
Sir Andrew:	And your horse now would make him an ass.
Maria:	Ass, I doubt not.

3 Modern critics identify Shakespeare's later comedies as 'Romances'. These include *The Winter's Tale*, *Pericles*, *Cymbeline* and *The Tempest*. They often involve magic, mystery, transformation, forgiveness and people being lost and found.

Look up the plots of these plays and see how they reflect this.

How has the popular meaning of the words tragedy, comedy, history and romance changed in modern times?

How did I do?

✓

I know that Shakespeare's plays can be divided into tragedies (including conflict and deaths), comedies (including confusion and a happy ending) and histories (focusing on royalty and patriotism). ☐

I know that some comedies have mystical elements and are now called romances. ☐

Teacher's tips

When you answer question 1 and question 2, look carefully at the words in each extract. Are there any dramatic exclamations or repetitions that sound like a tragedy? Are there words that indicate a historical event? Are there humorous lines or words that suggest a comedy?

43: Plot and themes: comedy

In this unit you will explore:
- the plots of Shakespeare's comedies
- the themes of Shakespeare's comedies.

Get started

Shakespeare's comedies often have quite tangled plots. The main plot is often mirrored by a subplot. A typical comedy can be divided into four main stages.

a **Trigger**: the action that sets off the main events.
b **Development**: characters fall in love, disguise themselves and set schemes in motion.
c **Chaos**: the schemes lead to mounting confusion.
d **Resolution**: confusions become clear, disguises are thrown off, everyone (almost) is happy. There may be marriages.

Typical themes in Shakespeare's comedies include: love, authority, appearance v. reality, change.

Practice

Here is Duke Orsino's opening speech in *Twelfth Night*.

> If music be the food of love, play on;
> Give me excess of it, that, surfeiting,
> The appetite may sicken, and so die.
> That strain again! It had a dying fall:
> O, it came o'er my ear like the sweet sound,
> That breathes upon a bank of violets,
> Stealing and giving odour! Enough; no more:
> 'Tis not so sweet now as it was before.
>
> (*Twelfth Night*, Act 1, scene 1)

1. What does this tell you about the likely themes of the play?
2. What kind of image is 'food of love', and what does it mean?
3. What is it that both steals and gives odour (perfume)?
4. What do you learn about Orsino here?

Challenge

5. The boxes on the next page show the plot of *Twelfth Night*, arranged in the five acts of the play but in the wrong order. The main plot is shown in red, the subplot in blue. What is the correct order?
6. What features of this plot make it typical of Shakespeare's comedies?
7. What are the similarities and differences between the main plot and subplot?

a   Sir Toby Belch and his friends have a party. Malvolio, the kill-joy steward, complains. Maria says she will forge love letters to trick Malvolio into thinking his mistress Olivia is in love with him. Olivia rejects Orsino. Malvolio is tricked.

b   Orsino and Viola are to marry. Toby marries Maria. Malvolio is let out of prison.

c   Orsino is love-sick for Olivia. Twins Viola and Sebastian are shipwrecked. Each thinks that the other is dead. Viola disguises herself as a young man, 'Cesario'. Orsino gets 'Cesario' to court Olivia on his behalf but Olivia falls in love with 'Cesario' and Viola falls in love with Orsino.

d   'Cesario' rejects Olivia. Sebastian and his friend Antonio turn up. Malvolio tries to woo Olivia. She thinks he's gone mad. Sir Andrew is tricked by Toby into challenging 'Cesario'. Antonio mistakes Viola (dressed as a man) for Sebastian and is arrested.

e   Sir Andrew hits Sebastian (in the belief that he is 'Cesario') and is shocked when Sebastian fights back. Olivia gets engaged to Sebastian.

Read the following passage from *A Midsummer Night's Dream*:

Demetrius: Do I entice you? Do I speak you fair?
    Or, rather, do I not in plainest truth
    Tell you, I do not, nor I cannot love you?

Helena: And even for that do I love you the more.
    I am your spaniel; and, Demetrius,
    The more you beat me, I will fawn on you:
    Use me but as your spaniel, spurn me, strike me,
    Neglect me, lose me; only give me leave,
    Unworthy as I am, to follow you.
    What worser place can I beg in your love, –
    And yet a place of high respect with me, –
    Than to be used as you use your dog?

Demetrius: Tempt not too much the hatred of my spirit;
    For I am sick when I do look on thee.

Helena: And I am sick when I look not on you.
            (*A Midsummer Night's Dream*, Act 2, scene 1)

8   How do you think this relationship turns out? Check your answer. Find Demetrius' speech in Act 4, scene 1, following the speech by Egeus beginning: 'Enough, enough, my lord.'

9   What themes can you identify here?

10 Lysander says: 'The course of true love never did run smooth' (Act 1, scene 1). How do you think the play reflects this?

How did I do?

I know that Shakespeare's comedies contain trickery, disguises, confusion, love and marriage, and all have happy endings. ☐

I know that common themes in Shakespeare's comedies are love, loyalty, confusion and authority. ☐

Teacher's tips

When you answer question 2, think about whether Shakespeare is being literal. Is he stating that one thing is actually another in order to create an image in the readers' minds? What does his comparison suggest about love?

44: Characterisation in a tragedy

In this unit you will explore:
- the characters in Shakespeare's tragedies
- how these characters are revealed.

Get started

Shakespeare's tragic characters are revealed in a number of ways.

- What they do
- What they say to other characters
- What other characters say about them
- Their *soliloquies* – solo speeches as if thinking aloud.

His characters include tragic heroes and heroines, other brave and noble characters, and fools or jokers who provide comic relief.

Practice

Shakespeare's characters always speak the truth in their soliloquies, and in *asides* (lines that other characters onstage are supposed not to hear). Read the following, taken from Hamlet's most famous soliloquy:

> To be, or not to be: that is the question:
> Whether 'tis nobler in the mind to suffer
> The slings and arrows of outrageous fortune,
> Or to take arms against a sea of troubles,
> And by opposing end them? To die: to sleep;
> No more . . .
>
> (*Hamlet*, Act 3, scene 1)

1. What kind of image does Hamlet use twice in lines 3–4, and what is the effect?
2. What does 'outrageous fortune' mean?
3. What is Hamlet thinking of doing?
4. Put these lines into plain modern English.

Challenge

In *Macbeth*, Lady Macbeth is ambitious and goads Macbeth to murder King Duncan so that Macbeth and she can become king and queen. When Macbeth decides he is not going to kill the king, she gets him to change his mind. Read her speech.

> When you durst* do it, then you were a man;
> And, to be more than what you were, you would
> Be so much more the man. Nor time nor place
> Did then adhere*, and yet you would make both:
> They have made themselves*, and that their fitness now
> Does unmake you. I have given suck, and know
> How tender 'tis to love the babe that milks me:
> I would, while it was smiling in my face,
> Have pluck'd my nipple from his boneless gums,
> And dash'd the brains out, had I so sworn as you
> Have done to this.
>
> *dared to
>
> *Neither the time nor place were suitable
> *The time and place are now right
>
> (*Macbeth*, Act 1, scene 7)

5 How does she appeal to Macbeth's pride in the first few lines?

6 Why does she talk about killing her baby?

7 What do you learn about Lady Macbeth's character from this speech? (Hint: Macbeth has not actually 'sworn' to kill Duncan.)

Later in the play, Macbeth and his wife, now king and queen, have a feast, at which Macbeth alone can see the ghost of a friend he has murdered – Banquo. He addresses the ghost:

> What man dare, I dare:
> Approach thou like the rugged Russian bear,
> The arm'd rhinoceros, or the Hyrcan tiger;
> Take any shape but that, and my firm nerves
> Shall never tremble: or be alive again,
> And dare me to the desert with thy sword;
> If trembling I inhabit then, protest me
> The baby of a girl. Hence, horrible shadow!
> Unreal mockery, hence!
> (GHOST OF BANQUO *vanishes*)
> Why, so: being gone,
> I am a man again.
>
> (*Macbeth*, Act 3, scene 4)

8 From this speech, what do you think Macbeth prides himself on?

9 Why is Macbeth afraid? Think of two reasons.

10 How do you think Macbeth and his wife differ?

Taking it further

Macbeth is corrupted, but some characters are villains from the start. Read Edmund's speech in *King Lear*, Act 1, scene 2, from 'Why brand they us' to 'Now, gods, stand up for bastards!' Compare him with Macbeth.

How did I do?

	✓
I know that Shakespeare's tragedies contain heroes and (a few) heroines, and some complete villains.	☐
I know that the characters are revealed in action and speech.	☐
I know that characters always speak the truth in soliloquies and in asides.	☐

Teacher's tips

When answering question 10 it may help you to think about what Macbeth feels when he sees the ghost of his friend, whom he killed.

45: Values in a history play

In this unit you will explore:
- how Shakespeare's histories deal with kingship
- the ideal king in Shakespeare's histories
- what personal qualities Shakespeare's histories promote.

Get started

Shakespeare's histories are based on historical events. They all focus on kingship and on the nation's need for order.

In his histories, Shakespeare expresses values (moral standards) relating to kingship and society. The king is seen as being divinely appointed, and responsible for bringing order to the nation – even if this means fighting a war first. Ideally, he should also be virtuous, an example to his people – though not all of Shakespeare's kings are good!

Practice

1 Match the words below with their meanings. If you're stuck, find the words in the first passage in the **Challenge** section and see if that helps.

Shakespeare's word	Meaning
purpose	breaking a promise
spotless, unspotted	intend, plan
arbitrement	defence, safeguard
peradventure	decision by contest (e.g. by a battle)
perjury	bloodied, wounded
bulwark	guiltless, innocent
gored	perhaps

Challenge

Read the extracts below and answer the questions that follow each one.

In Extract **a**, King Henry V talks about the responsibility of a king. In Extract **b**, he says that kings have a hard life. In Extract **c**, his father, Henry IV, says that it is hard for kings to sleep.

a

. . . the king is not bound to answer the particular endings of his soldiers, the father of his son, nor the master of his servant; for they purpose not their death, when they purpose their services. Besides, there is no king, be his cause never so spotless, if it come to the arbitrement of swords, can try it out with all unspotted soldiers: some peradventure have on them the guilt of premeditated and contrived murder; some, of beguiling virgins with the broken seals of perjury; some, making the wars their bulwark, that have before gored the gentle bosom of peace with pillage and robbery.

(*Henry V*, Act 4, scene 1)

2 What is Henry saying about a king's responsibility towards his people?

3 Of what kinds of immoral behaviour does Henry say his men may be guilty?

b

Upon the king! Let us our lives, our souls,
Our debts, our careful wives,
Our children and our sins lay on the king!
We must bear all. O hard condition,
Twin-born with greatness, subject to the breath
Of every fool, whose sense no more can feel
But his own wringing*! What infinite heart's-ease   *stomach ache
Must kings neglect, that private men enjoy!
And what have kings, that privates* have not too,   *ordinary men
Save ceremony*, save general ceremony?   *the signs of respect given to a king, e.g.
And what art thou, thou idle ceremony?   everyone bowing
What kind of god art thou, that suffer'st more
Of mortal griefs than do thy worshippers?
What are thy rents? What are thy comings in?
O ceremony, show me but thy worth!

(*Henry V*, Act 4, scene 1)

4 Who does Henry imagine speaking the sentence beginning 'Let us . . .'?

5 When he says 'We must bear all', who does he mean by 'We'?

6 How much does Henry value 'ceremony'?

7 What does he think, overall, of being a king?

Taking it further

Read the opening speech of Shakespeare's *Richard III* and compare Richard with Henry V. Who is the better king?

Make notes on what you think Shakespeare's attitude towards kings was.

c

Canst thou, O partial sleep, give thy repose
To the wet sea-boy in an hour so rude,
And in the calmest and most stillest night,
With all appliances and means to boot,
Deny it to a king? Then happy low, lie down!
Uneasy lies the head that wears a crown.

(*Henry IV, Part 1*, Act 3, scene 1)

8 Henry IV thinks that sleep unfairly favours (is 'partial' towards) the poor, such as the wet sailor boy. What point is he making about kingship?

How did I do?

	✓
I know that Shakespeare's histories focus on the importance of having a strong, virtuous king to bring order.	☐
I know that Shakespeare saw kings as appointed by God, but still human.	☐
I know that Shakespeare felt that kings have responsibilities.	☐

Teacher's tips

When you answer question 5, think about how royal people refer to themselves. To answer question 8, look closely at the last line of Henry IV's speech.

46: Planning an essay on a theme

In this unit you will explore:
- how to plan an essay on a theme.

Get started

Planning an essay involves considering what to include and how to organise your ideas. Themes are key ideas and messages in a text.

Practice

1 Think about the storylines in each of the following well-known tales and then make a list of the themes in each.

- a Snow White
- b Hansel and Gretel
- c Goldilocks
- d Jack and the Beanstalk

For example, Cinderella is about a poor girl who is mistreated by her stepfamily, and visited by her fairy godmother. She goes to a ball and eventually marries a charming prince.

The themes are love, family life, sibling rivalry and the rich–poor divide.

Challenge

Themes can appear through plot, characters and repeated ideas or images. Read this blurb about the novel *Abomination* by Robert Swindells.

> Martha is different. She longs to have friends and to be accepted by her class-mates, but her parents belong to a strict religious group which means no computers, no TV, no trendy clothes, and no friends. Taunted and bullied at school, and lonely at home, Martha knows there has to be some other way of living, but what? Martha has a secret. Its name is Abomination, and it must never be discovered. Will she ever reveal the secret that keeps her trapped?

2 What do you think the themes are in this book?

3 Which words or phrases in the blurb suggest this?

Themes can appear through plot and characters but also through repeated ideas or images. Sometimes, themes can also be apparent because of the form or structure of a text, so in a war poem a lack of organised structure may represent the chaos of war. Imagery and form are particularly relevant when we look at poetry.

Read the following poem by William Blake. It's called 'The Garden of Love' and it is taken from his *Songs of Experience*.

> I went to the Garden of Love,
> And saw what I never had seen;
> A Chapel was built in the midst,
> Where I used to play on the green.
>
> And the gates of this Chapel were shut,
> And 'Thou shalt not' writ over the door;
> So I turned to the Garden of Love
> That so many sweet flowers bore.
>
> And I saw it was filled with graves,
> And tombstones where flowers should be;
> And priests in black gowns were walking their rounds,
> And binding with briars my joys and desires.

4 Identify any repeated words. What is their effect?

5 Find as many negative words as you can.

6 Research William Blake and find out what his attitude to religion was.

7 From the poem, make a list of images related to religion.

8 What do you think Blake is saying about religion in this poem?

Look at how the poem is organised.

9 In the last stanza, which words does Blake use to create internal rhyme?

10 How could this rhyme and the structure of the poem as a whole suggest a lack of freedom and how does this relate to Blake's views on religion?

11 Create a spidergram on the theme of religion in this poem. Include some quotations to support your ideas. It could start like this:

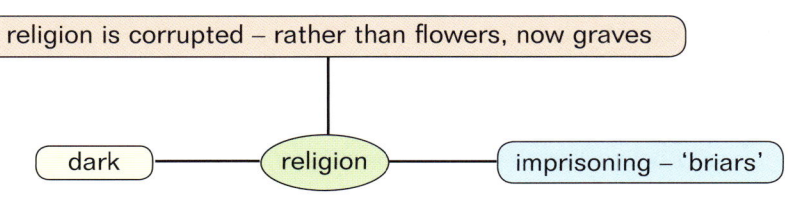

- religion is corrupted – rather than flowers, now graves
- dark
- religion
- imprisoning – 'briars'

12 Use this diagram to help you plan an essay entitled 'Examine how the theme of religion is presented in "The Garden of Love".' Decide what points you will include in your essay and the order in which they will appear.

Taking it further

This poem is a counterpart to 'The Echoing Green' – a poem in Blake's *Songs of Innocence*. Read this poem and do as you have done with the poem printed above. Look for repeated images and ideas.

Plan an essay comparing the themes that appear in these two poems.

How did I do?

- I know that to plan an essay on a theme, it is important to identify the themes in the text.
- I know that themes appear in the plot; in what characters say, do and think; and in repeated images or ideas.
- I know that planning an essay on a theme involves brainstorming ideas about the theme, finding evidence and organising my points.

Teacher's tips

When you answer question 9, look specifically at the last two lines and read these aloud. Listen out for words that sound similar to each other. When you decide on the order of your points for question 12, think carefully about which points would follow on from one another easily.

47: Writing an essay on a theme

In this unit you will explore:
- how to write a draft essay on a theme.

Get started

When you write an essay you need to structure your ideas and explain and analyse your evidence. You also need to use formal language. Drafting an essay involves you testing out ideas and words. You may have to rewrite sections to improve the essay.

Practice

1 Match the informal words and phrases listed below with their more formal equivalents.

Informal	More formal
get across	character
show	repeats
person in the story	contrasts
says again	portray
beat	convey
writes the opposite	rhythm

Challenge

In the previous unit, you planned an essay on the theme of religion in 'The Garden of Love'. Now, you will start to draft and write your essay.

Look back at the spidergram and essay plan that you created in Unit 14. Remind yourself that an essay is made up of an **introduction**, **main body** and **conclusion**.

2 An **introduction** should outline the main points you will cover in the rest of your essay. Read the two examples of introductions to this essay below. Which introduction do you think is better? Why?

a In this poem Blake writes about religion. He says that it is corrupt and stops you from being free. He writes using a regular rhyme and this helps to suggest the tight control religion has over you.

b In 'The Garden of Love', Blake presents religion as cruel and corrupt. The poem, a counterpart to one of his Songs of Innocence, shows what happens when innocence is lost. Things change. The world that was once alive and joyous is replaced with a world of darkness and death.

3 Do both of these introductions have some good parts?

4 Use some of these ideas and your own to write your introduction to your essay.

The **main body** of an essay is made up of several paragraphs, each dealing with a separate point. Each paragraph should start with a topic sentence and provide evidence and analysis.

Read the two paragraphs that follow. Each refers to the novel *Pride and Prejudice* by Jane Austen.

> **a** It is evident from the first sentence that the theme of marriage is an important part of the novel. Austen writes 'It is a truth universally acknowledged that a single man in possession of a good fortune must be in want of a wife'. Not only is the theme of marriage important, but the fact that money plays its part in marriage at this time is also clear. Mrs Bennet's insistence that her husband visit Mr Bingley to secure an invitation and hopefully a husband for one of her daughters proves that for women of the eighteen hundreds, marriage and money went hand in hand.
>
> **b** Marriage is a key theme in the book. Austen opens her novel with a famous line: 'It is a truth universally acknowledged that a single man in possession of a good fortune must be in want of a wife' and this shows how important marriage is in the novel. Everyone knows it – it is 'universally acknowledged', as Austen says. How different characters see marriage is what I will now look at.

5 Which paragraph do you consider to be the better? Why?

6 Look back at these two paragraphs and identify where the main point is made, where there is evidence from the text and where there is analysis.

7 Does either of these paragraphs develop its point or ideas? How?

8 Now, write your main body. Make sure you make a point, support it with evidence and analyse your evidence. Also make sure you stick to the question! Don't start to write a summary of the book.

A **conclusion** comes at the end of the essay. It sums up the main points, without repeating the introduction, and it shows that your ideas have developed. You might include your reactions to the author's or poet's treatment of a theme in this paragraph too.

9 Write your conclusion, then check and improve your essay draft.

How did I do?

	✓
I know that to write a critical essay on a theme, it is necessary to plan and list points, and to collect evidence from the text.	☐
I know that the essay should be shaped by using an introduction, main body and conclusion.	☐
I know that it is necessary to quote from the text and to analyse the evidence, relating it to the question.	☐

Teacher's tips

When you write paragraphs in an essay, it is a good idea to start each paragraph with a *topic sentence*. This is a sentence that makes clear the focus of the paragraph. For example this starting sentence: *Marriage is a key theme in the novel Pride and Prejudice,* is a topic sentence.

48: Writing a playscript

In this unit you will explore:
- how to write the opening to a tragic play.

Get started

Tragedies are plays that unavoidably end in destruction and death. A playscript is written to be performed. It relies on action and dialogue to entertain an audience.

Practice

1 Which of the following well-known plays are tragedies?

- *Romeo and Juliet*
- *The Merchant of Venice*
- *Macbeth*
- *Much Ado about Nothing*
- *Twelfth Night*
- *Othello*
- *King Lear*
- *The Tempest*

Challenge

Read the following extracts taken from the openings of *Antigone* by Jean Anouilh and *A View from the Bridge* by Arthur Miller.

Antigone

Set without historical or geographical implications. Three identical doors. At curtain rise, all the characters are on stage, chatting, knitting, playing cards and so on. The PROLOGUE emerges from the rest and comes forward to speak.

Prologue: The people gathered here are about to act the story of Antigone. The one who's going to play the lead is the thin girl sitting there silent. Staring in front of her. Thinking. She's thinking that soon she's going to be Antigone. That she'll suddenly stop being the thin dark girl whose family didn't take her seriously and rise up against everyone. Against Creon, her uncle the king. She's thinking she's going to die . . . though she's still young, and like everyone else would have preferred to live.

But there's nothing to be done. Her name is Antigone, and she's going to have to play her part right through to the end.

Ever since the play started she has felt herself hurtling further and further away from her sister Ismene. (That's her chatting and laughing with a young man over there.) Further and further away from all the rest of us, who are just here to watch, and haven't got to die in a few hours' time.

A View from the Bridge

Alfieri: . . . Justice is very important here.

But this is Red Hook, not Sicily. This is the slum that faces the bay on the seaward side of Brooklyn Bridge. This is the gullet of New York swallowing the tonnage of the world. And now we are quite civilised, quite American. Now we settle for half and I like it better. I no longer keep a pistol in my filing cabinet.

And my practice is entirely unromantic.

My wife has warned me, so have my friends; they tell me the people in this neighbourhood lack elegance, glamour. After all who have I dealt with in my life? Longshoremen and their wives, and fathers and grandfathers, compensation cases, evictions, family squabbles – the petty troubles of the poor – and yet . . . every few years there is still a case and as the parties tell me what the trouble is, the flat air in my office suddenly washes in with the green scent of the sea, the dust in this air is blown away and the thought comes that in some Caesar's year, in Calabria perhaps or on the cliff at Syracuse, another lawyer, quite differently dressed heard the same complaint and sat there as powerless as I and watched it run its bloody course.

2 Research Greek tragedies and find out who Sophocles was and what a chorus was.

3 Using this new information, note the ways in which Prologue and Alfieri act as choruses.

4 Find words and phrases from these two openings that establish the plays as tragedies that will end unhappily.

5 What words and phrases suggest that fate will contribute to the tragic outcomes of the plays?

6 Find examples of where the playwrights use repetition.

7 Both playwrights make their openings sound poetic. Identify any examples of metaphor and explain their effect. Also look for any other poetic devices that they use.

8 What examples of contrast can you see in both extracts?

9 How do the playwrights make their plays sound weighty? How do they give their plays gravitas?

10 You are going to write the opening to a tragedy, using some of the techniques Miller and Anouilh use.

   a Firstly, decide on a central character whose life will be most affected by fate. Consider how and why this is. Is he or she a common person or someone important?
   b Then, create a spidergram of ideas for your setting.

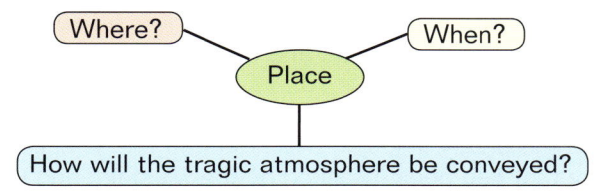

   ```
        Where?           When?
              \         /
               Place
                 |
   How will the tragic atmosphere be conveyed?
   ```

   c Decide whether you will have a choral character like Alfieri in your opening.
   d Write your opening. Remember to use some poetic devices, repetition and contrast.

Taking it further

Read the opening to a translation of the original Greek play *Antigone*.

Write a soliloquy for your tragic character to add to the opening you have already written.

How did I do?

☐ I know that tragic plays are staged performances in which characters face hardships brought upon them by gods and fate.

☐ I know that tragedies often feature choruses and end in death or destruction.

Teacher's tips

When you answer question 9, look at the topics/subjects being discussed by the speakers. Do the speakers refer to things that are great and beyond every day occurrences?

49: Writing to create a mood

In this unit you will explore:
- how to write a descriptive passage which creates a certain mood or atmosphere.

Get started

Atmosphere is created through a writer's choice of vocabulary and imagery.

Practice

1. Brainstorm any connotations that spring to mind when you read each of the following words.

   a devastation
   b carcasses
   c bloodstained
   d procession
   e wrecks

Challenge

Read the following taken from J. G. Ballard's *Empire of the Sun*. In this passage, a group of British prisoners are marching across Japanese-occupied China.

All afternoon they moved northwards across the plain of the Whangoo River, through the maze of creeks and canals that separated the paddy fields. Lunghua Airfield fell behind them, and the apartment houses of the French Concession rose like advertisement hoardings in the August sunlight. The river was a few hundred yards to their right, its brown surface broken by the wrecks of patrol boats and motorized junks that sat in the shallows.

Here in the approaches to the Nantao district, the devastation caused by the American bombing lay on all sides. Craters like circular swimming pools covered the paddy fields, in which floated the carcasses of water buffaloes. They passed the remains of a convoy that had been attacked by the Mustang and Lightning fighters. A line of military trucks and staff cars sat under trees as if dismantled in an outdoor workshop. Wheels, doors and axles were scattered around vehicles whose fenders and body panels had been torn away by the cannon fire.

Swarms of flies rose from bloodstained windshields as the prisoners stopped to relieve themselves. A few steps behind Jim, Mr Maxted left the procession and sat on the running board of an ammunition wagon. Still carrying his case, Jim went back for him.

'We're nearly there, Mr Maxted. I can smell the docks.'

2. Ballard uses carefully chosen vocabulary in this passage. Which word in the opening sentence make the canals and creeks sound many and winding?

3. Identify any similes and explain their effect.

4. Find words and phrases that suggest the landscape has been scarred by war.

A technique that writers use to make their writing more evocative is to avoid the verb 'was' or 'is' and use more direct and active verbs. For example, rather than writing 'Lunghua Airfield was behind them', Ballard writes 'Lunghua Airfield *fell* behind them'.

5 Identify other examples of verbs that Ballard uses to good effect.

6 Besides using verbs, what other parts of speech does Ballard use to aid his description?

7 What mood does Ballard create in this opening to a chapter?

Read the following paragraph, also taken from *Empire of the Sun*. Some of the words have been omitted.

8 What words would be effective in the spaces?

> A _____ morning sun filled the stadium, reflected in the _____ of water that covered the athletic track, and in the _____ radiators of the American cars parked behind the goal posts at the northern end of the football pitch. Supporting himself against Mr Maxted's shoulder, Jim _____ the hundreds of men and women lying on the _____ grass. A few prisoners _____ on the ground, their sunburnt but _____ faces like _____ _____ . They stared at the cars, suspicious of their _____ _____ , with _____ eyes.

9 Imagine a scene with a certain mood that you will describe. You might choose to describe a war-torn place or somewhere happier. Whichever you decide on, remember to write in a precise way and to employ some comparisons.

Taking it further

Read J.G. Ballard's novel *Empire of the Sun* and then read W.H. Auden's poem 'Refugee Blues'.

Describe a concentration camp from the point of view of a prisoner who has been in one.

How did I do?

✓

☐ I know that evocative writing suggests a mood because of the writer's careful selection of imagery and vocabulary.

☐ I know that when writing a moody piece, it is necessary to use active verbs, precise adjectives and nouns, and to include some comparisons.

Teacher's tips

Remember, **parts of speech** are the categories that words fall into such as *adjectives, nouns, adverbs,* and so on.

50: Writing in role

In this unit you will explore:
- how to write in the voice of a Shakespearean character.

Get started

Writing in the voice of a character requires you to take on the thoughts and feelings of that character and to use his or her language as far as possible. Shakespeare lived and wrote in Elizabethan times – around 1600. This is relevant to how his characters think and feel.

Practice

1. Look at the list of Shakespearean words below and find out what they mean.

   a rated
   b usance
   c cur
   d gaberdine
   e rheum
   f ducat
   g thine
   h thee

   (Hint: look them up on a Shakespeare website if necessary.)

Challenge

Read this extract taken from *The Merchant of Venice*. In it, Shakespeare reflects beliefs at the time towards Jews. Here we see Shylock, a Jew, approached by Antonio, who wants to borrow money from him.

Shylock

Signor Antonio, many a time and oft
In the Rialto* you have rated me
About my moneys and my usances:
Still have I borne it with a patient shrug,
For sufferance is the badge of all our tribe.
You call me misbeliever, cut-throat dog,
And spit upon my Jewish gaberdine,
And all for use of that which is mine own.
Well then, it now appears you need my help:
Go to, then; you come to me, and you say
'Shylock, we would have moneys:' you say so;
You, that did void your rheum upon my beard
And foot me as you spurn a stranger cur
Over your threshold: moneys is your suit
What should I say to you? Should I not say
'Hath a dog money? Is it possible
A cur can lend three thousand ducats?' Or

*Rialto – stock exchange

Shall I bend low and in a bondman's key,
With bated breath and whispering humbleness,
   Say this;
'Fair sir, you spit on me on Wednesday last;
You spurn'd me such a day; another time
You call'd me dog; and for these courtesies
I'll lend you thus much moneys'?

Antonio

I am as like to call thee so again,
To spit on thee again, to spurn thee too.
If thou wilt lend this money, lend it not
As to thy friends; for when did friendship take
A breed for barren metal of his friend?
But lend it rather to thine enemy,
Who, if he break, thou mayst with better face
Exact the penalty.

(*The Merchant of Venice*, Act 1, scene 3)

2 Look at line 3 of Shylock's speech. What has Antonio criticised Shylock about previously?

3 What animal does Shylock say Antonio has compared him to? Find three references to this.

4 Find two examples of lines that show that Shylock is upset and angry at the way he has been treated by Antonio in the past.

5 Which line suggests that Shylock's unhappiness is not just about his own personal mistreatment but that of many?

6 Antonio admits that his attitude to Shylock will not change, but what suggestion does he make to Shylock about lending the money to him?

7 In what tone do you think the last line in Shylock's speech should be delivered and why?

Just after this, Shylock agrees to lend Antonio the money on the condition that if he fails to repay it on a specified date, Shylock may remove a pound of flesh from any part of Antonio's body he chooses.

8 Why do you think Shylock does this?

9 Make a list of the thoughts and feelings that contributed to Shylock's decision.

10 Imagine that you are Shylock. After your meeting with Antonio and his agreement to your terms of contract, you return home and write a diary entry which recounts what has happened and also indicates how you feel about things and what your thoughts are. Try to use some of Shakespeare's language.

Taking it further

Find a copy of *The Merchant of Venice* (either in a book or by searching for 'Complete Works Shakespeare' on the internet). If you can, read the whole play. Otherwise, just read Act 4, scene 1 up to the point when judgement has been made and Shylock exits. (Go to nfs.sparknotes.com if you need help in understanding the language of the text.)

Imagine that you are Shylock at this point. Write a letter to your dead wife telling her of your troubles, thoughts and feelings.

How did I do?

✔

I know that writing in the voice of a character from literature means taking on his or her thoughts and feelings, and recounting events that have happened to him or her. ☐

I know that when writing as a Shakespearean character I should be aware of beliefs at the time and how people spoke in the Elizabethan era. ☐

Teacher's tips

You may find it useful to watch a film version of *The Merchant of Venice* or go to the theatre to watch the play. This will help you to see and hear how Shylock feels.

51: Narrative voice

In this unit you will explore:
- narrative voice – the person telling the story
- how to write using different narrative voices.

Get started

Writers make choices about how to tell a story and through whom. They might write in the first person – from a main character's point of view (I, me, my) or in the third person – as if events are being reported to us (he, she, they).

This use of third person could be from a limited point of view (where only one character's thoughts and feelings are known) or from a third person omniscient view (where the narrator sees everything and knows what is going on in all characters' heads).

Practice

1 Read the following sentences taken from novels. Which are written in the first and which in the third person?

- **a** My favourite time is after dinner when I have the place to myself.
- **b** His mouth encountered gravel and he spat frantically, afraid that some of his teeth had been knocked out.
- **c** He was waiting for us, in fact, at the public-house; and asked me how I found myself, like an old acquaintance.
- **d** Naledi stared out of the window without seeing anything.

Challenge

Read this extract from Charles Dickens' novel *Oliver Twist*.

'Will you go along with me, Oliver?' said Mr Bumble, in a majestic voice.
   Oliver was about to say that he would go along with anybody with great readiness, when, glancing upward, he caught sight of Mrs Mann, who had got behind the beadle's chair, and was shaking her fist at him with a furious countenance. He took the hint at once, for the fist had been too often impressed upon his body not to be deeply impressed upon his recollection.
   'Will she go with me?' inquired poor Oliver.
   'No, she can't,' replied Mr Bumble. 'But she'll come and see you sometimes.'
   This was no very great consolation to the child. Young as he was, however, he had sense enough to make a feint of feeling great regret at going away. It was no very difficult matter for the boy to call tears into his eyes. Hunger and recent ill-usage are great assistants if you want to cry; and Oliver cried very naturally indeed.

2 What sort of narrative voice is used here – first or third person?

Read this extract from Jane Austen's novel *Pride and Prejudice*, written using an omniscient narrator.

> In a few days Mr Bingley returned Mr Bennet's visit, and sat about ten minutes with him in his library. He had entertained hopes of being admitted to a sight of the young ladies, of whose beauty he had heard much; but he saw only the father. The ladies were somewhat more fortunate, for they had the advantage of ascertaining from an upper window that he wore a blue coat, and rode a black horse.

3 How do you know the narrator is omniscient?

4 Rewrite this passage in the third person but with a limited narrative voice.

5 Why do you think writers might choose to write in the first person? What benefits does this have over third person? What disadvantages does this have?

Read the following short extract taken from Emily Brontë's novel *Wuthering Heights*.

> While leading the way upstairs she recommended that I should hide the candle, and not make a noise, for her master had an odd notion about the chamber* she would put me in and never let anybody lodge there willingly. I asked the reason. She did not know, she answered: she had only lived there a year or two and they had so many queer goings on she could not begin to be curious.
>   Too stupefied* to be curious myself, I fastened my door and glanced round for the bed.
>
>   *chamber* – room
>   *stupefied* – dazed

6 What do you think the narrator's thoughts and feelings are as she follows the lady?

7 Continue this story, using first person narration. Write about fifteen lines.

Taking it further

Experiment with your story. Write it using third person and third person omniscient narration and see which version you like best.

How did I do?

	✓
I know that writers use different narrative voices to reflect different points of view.	☐
I know that a writer can bias a reader towards or against characters by choosing a particular narrative voice.	☐
I know that writers can use a first, limited third or omniscient third person voice.	☐

Teacher's tips

Writing in the first person is often seen as a more personal way of writing. It lets readers get closer to characters, and experience events from their points of view.

52: A science fiction experiment

In this unit you will explore:
- how to write in the science fiction genre.

Get started

Science fiction is writing that is set in a world that is different from our own reality. It explores the impact of imagined science and technology on society and individuals.

Practice

1. Look at the list of words below and identify which you think sound as if they might belong in a science fiction novel.

| Captain Gus Eckert | throttle | bed | apple | pod | deck | grass |
| terrain | desk | table | surface | Heat-Ray | nutrition | |

Challenge

Read the following extract taken from H.G. Wells's *War of the Worlds*.

Quickly, one after the other, one, two, three, four of the armoured Martians appeared, far away over the little trees, across the flat meadows that stretched towards Chertsey, and striding hurriedly towards the river. Little cowled figures they seemed at first, going with a rolling motion and as fast as flying birds.

Then, advancing obliquely towards us, came a fifth. Their armoured bodies glittered in the sun as they swept swiftly forward upon the guns, growing rapidly larger as they drew nearer. One on the extreme left, the remotest that is, flourished a huge case high in the air, and the ghostly, terrible Heat-Ray I had already seen on Friday night smote towards Chertsey, and struck the town. At sight of these strange, swift, and terrible creatures the crowd near the water's edge seemed to me to be for a moment horror-struck. There was no screaming or shouting, but a silence. Then a hoarse murmur and a movement of feet – a splashing from the water. A man, too frightened to drop the portmanteau he carried on his shoulder, swung round and sent me staggering with a blow from the corner of his burden. A woman thrust at me with her hand and rushed past me. I turned with the rush of the people, but I was not too terrified for thought. The terrible Heat-Ray was in my mind. To get under water! That was it!

'Get under water!' I shouted, unheeded.

I faced about again, and rushed towards the approaching Martian, rushed right down the gravelly beach and headlong into the water. Others did the same. A boatload of people putting back came leaping out as I rushed past. The stones under my feet were muddy and slippery, and the river was so low that I ran perhaps twenty feet scarcely waist-deep. Then, as the Martian towered overhead scarcely a couple of hundred yards away, I flung myself forward under the surface. The splashes of the people in the boats leaping into the river sounded like thunderclaps in my ears. People were landing hastily on both sides of the river. But the Martian machine took no more notice for the moment of the people running this way and that than a man would of the confusion of ants in a nest against which his foot has kicked. When, half suffocated, I raised my head above water, the Martian's hood pointed at the batteries that were still firing across the river, and as it advanced it swung loose what must have been the generator of the Heat-Ray.

2 Describe the Martians.

3 What in the passage shows the fear and panic of the humans?

4 Find words or phrases that suggest the chaos of the scene.

5 Find examples of simile and metaphor in the extract and explain their effect.

6 Make a list of words and phrases that establish this as an extract from a science fiction novel.

7 Imagine a setting for a science fiction story that you will write. Create a spidergram of ideas related to this world.

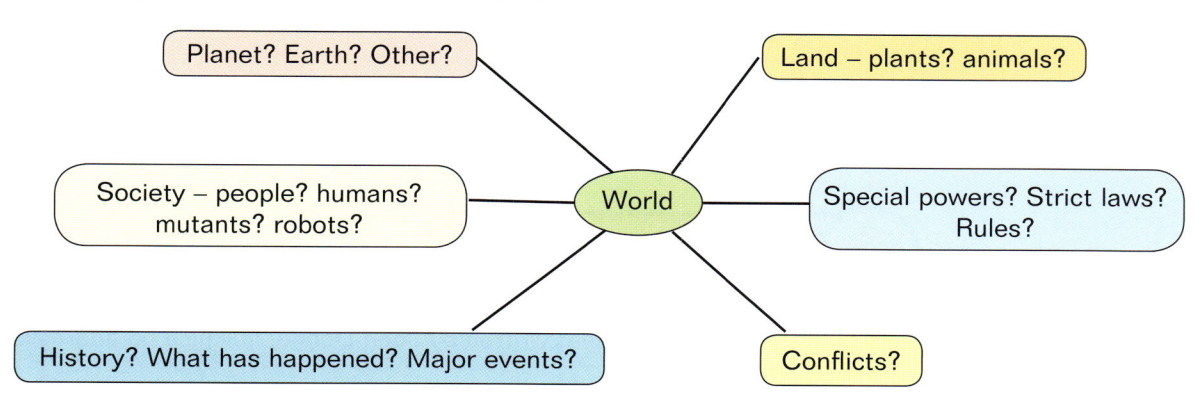

- Planet? Earth? Other?
- Land – plants? animals?
- Society – people? humans? mutants? robots?
- World
- Special powers? Strict laws? Rules?
- History? What has happened? Major events?
- Conflicts?

8 Write the opening to your science fiction short story by describing the setting – this imagined world. You could introduce a character to the story as well.

Taking it further

Look at the website dedicated to H.G. Wells's novel: www.war-oftheworlds.co.uk.

Develop your science fiction opening into a full-length short story. Think carefully about your plot before you commit yourself to paper.

How did I do?

- I know that science fiction is a genre that explores life in an imagined world, often set in the future. ✔
- I know that science fiction explores the impact of science and technology.
- I know that when writing science fiction, it is important to consider in detail the world in which the story will be set.

Teacher's tips

In 2005 Tom Cruise starred in a film version of *The War of the Worlds*. Why not watch this film to see how the director Steven Spielberg presented the science fiction genre?

53: Writing a sonnet

In this unit you will explore:
- how to write a sonnet.

Get started

A sonnet is a fourteen-line poem with a set rhyme scheme and rhythm.

Practice

1. Look on the internet to find out the difference between Shakespearean and Petrarchan sonnets.

2. Now define each of the following.

   a quatrain
   b octet
   c sestet
   d rhyming couplet

Challenge

Read the following sonnet written by John Donne, in which he addresses death itself.

```
x   /  x /    x   /   x  / x  /
```
Death be not proud, though some have called thee*
Mighty and dreadful, for thou* art not so,
For those whom thou think'st thou dost* overthrow,
Die not, poor death, nor yet canst thou kill me.
From rest and sleep, which but thy* pictures be,
Much pleasure, then from thee, much more must flow,
And soonest our best men with thee do go,
Rest of their bones, and soul's delivery.
Thou art slave to Fate, Chance, kings, and desperate men,
And dost with poison, war, and sickness dwell,
And poppy, or charms can make us sleep as well,
And better than thy stroke; why swell'st thou then?
One short sleep past, we wake eternally,
And death shall be no more; death, thou shalt die.

thee – you
thou – you
dost – do
thy – your
x   unstressed syllable
/   stressed syllable

3. Which words show that the poet is addressing death itself?

4. By talking to death as if it were human, what has the poet done?

5. Is this a Shakespearean or Petrarchan sonnet? How do you know?

6. The poem is written in a particular rhythm called iambic pentameter. What is this?

7. Write a line using this rhythm.

8. In the fifth line, to what does Donne compare death?

9. How does this comparison help the poet to develop his argument?

10. According to Donne, what causes death?

11. Why does Donne refer to 'poppy, or charms'? What is he saying here?

12. What point does the poet make in his concluding two lines?

13. Imagine that you are addressing an abstract concept like death – love, for example.

    a Create a spidergram about the points you would make to love about its nature.

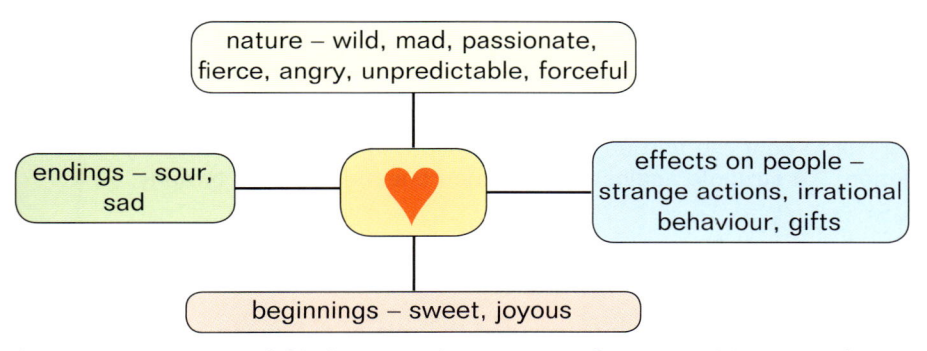

    - nature – wild, mad, passionate, fierce, angry, unpredictable, forceful
    - endings – sour, sad
    - effects on people – strange actions, irrational behaviour, gifts
    - beginnings – sweet, joyous

    (Hint: look at some of Shakespeare's sonnets – Sonnets 130, 137 and 147, for example – to help you. Copies can be found on the internet.)

    b Write the first quatrain of your sonnet. For example:

    > Love, you are mad, as men in hot chase
    > Stormy and flighty is what you become
    > Like passion and venom in a wild race
    > Sweet flowers, soft words, verses for some.

    c Now write the whole sonnet.

Taking it further

Read some early twentieth-century sonnets by Thomas Hardy at www.sonnets.org.

Write a sonnet imitating one of these.

How did I do?

	✔
I know that sonnets are poems that debate an idea or philosophise in some way.	☐
I know that when writing a sonnet I should think about rhythm and rhyme as well as the ideas.	☐

Teacher's tips

This is a tricky unit, so just try your best to answer the questions. The answers to the questions are found in chronological order in the poem.

54: Persuasive politics

In this unit you will explore:
- how to write a persuasive speech.

Get started

Persuasive speeches aim to influence people into feeling and thinking a particular way. They do this by using language that is emotive and that includes their audience.

Practice

1. Give the meaning for each of the following.

   a rhetorical question
   b emotive language
   c pronoun
   d allusion
   e pun
   f juxtaposition
   g alliteration
   h metaphor
   i rhyme
   j exaggeration
   k evidence
   l lists
   m contrast

Challenge

Read this extract from a speech by J.F. Kennedy, 35th president of America.

Now the trumpet summons us again – not as a call to bear arms, though arms we need – not as a call to battle, though embattled we are – but a call to bear the burden of a long twilight struggle, year in and year out, 'rejoicing in hope, patient in tribulation' – a struggle against the common enemies of man: tyranny, poverty, disease, and war itself.

Can we forge against these enemies a grand and global alliance, North and South, East and West, that can assure a more fruitful life for all mankind? Will you join in that historic effort?

In the long history of the world, only a few generations have been granted the role of defending freedom in its hour of maximum danger. I do not shrink from this responsibility – I welcome it. I do not believe that any of us would exchange places with any other people or any other generation. The energy, the faith, the devotion which we bring to this endeavour will light our country and all who serve it – and the glow from that fire can truly light the world.

And so, my fellow Americans: ask not what your country can do for you – ask what you can do for your country.

My fellow citizens of the world: ask not what America will do for you, but what together we can do for the freedom of man.

Finally, whether you are citizens of America or citizens of the world, ask of us here the same high standards of strength and sacrifice which we ask of you. With a good conscience our only sure reward, with history the final judge of our deeds, let us go forth to lead the land we love, asking His blessing and His help, but knowing that here on earth God's work must truly be our own.

2. Look at the first paragraph of the extract. What metaphors can you see and what do you understand from them?

3. What evidence is there in the first paragraph of Kennedy using contrasting words/ideas?

4. Look at how Kennedy ended his opening paragraph. What device did he use and for what effect?

5. In the second paragraph Kennedy made his audience feel included. How?

6. How did he end his second paragraph and what is the effect of this?

7. Make a list of any other persuasive lines from the extract and explain what devices the president used in these.

8. Imagine that you are a politician who is promoting a Utopian (perfect) world. Write your election speech. Remember to make your opening engaging and don't forget to use some persuasive devices.

   (Hint: think about what your Utopia would include and what it would have abolished. These will form the basis of some of the contrasts you will include in your election speech.)

Taking it further

Search the internet for speeches to read and listen to. Listen to Martin Luther King's 'I Have a Dream' speech.

Imagine that you are Martin Luther King, and write a speech about the world as it is today.

How did I do?

	✓
I know that a persuasive speech appeals to an audience's emotions.	☐
I know that a persuasive speech tries to get the audience to adopt the speaker's views.	☐
I know that rhetorical questions, emotive language, contrasts and personal pronouns can be used to make a speech effective.	☐

Teacher's tips

If you're uncertain what any of the words in question 1 mean, you can always use a dictionary! For question 5, look carefully at the *pronouns* that Kennedy uses in the second paragraph of the extract.

55: An enticing leaflet

In this unit you will explore:
- leaflets that provide the public with information
- how to write a leaflet about a place of interest.

Get started

Leaflets can have the purpose of informing, advising or persuading. A leaflet about a place of interest is likely to be informative and persuasive, and should attract readers.

Practice

1. Look at the list of places below. If a leaflet about each place were produced, who do you think would be the target audience for each leaflet?

   a A school classroom
   b Thorpe Park
   c Your house
   d The M25 motorway
   e Buckingham Palace
   f London Dungeons
   g The local theatre

Challenge

Look at this leaflet:

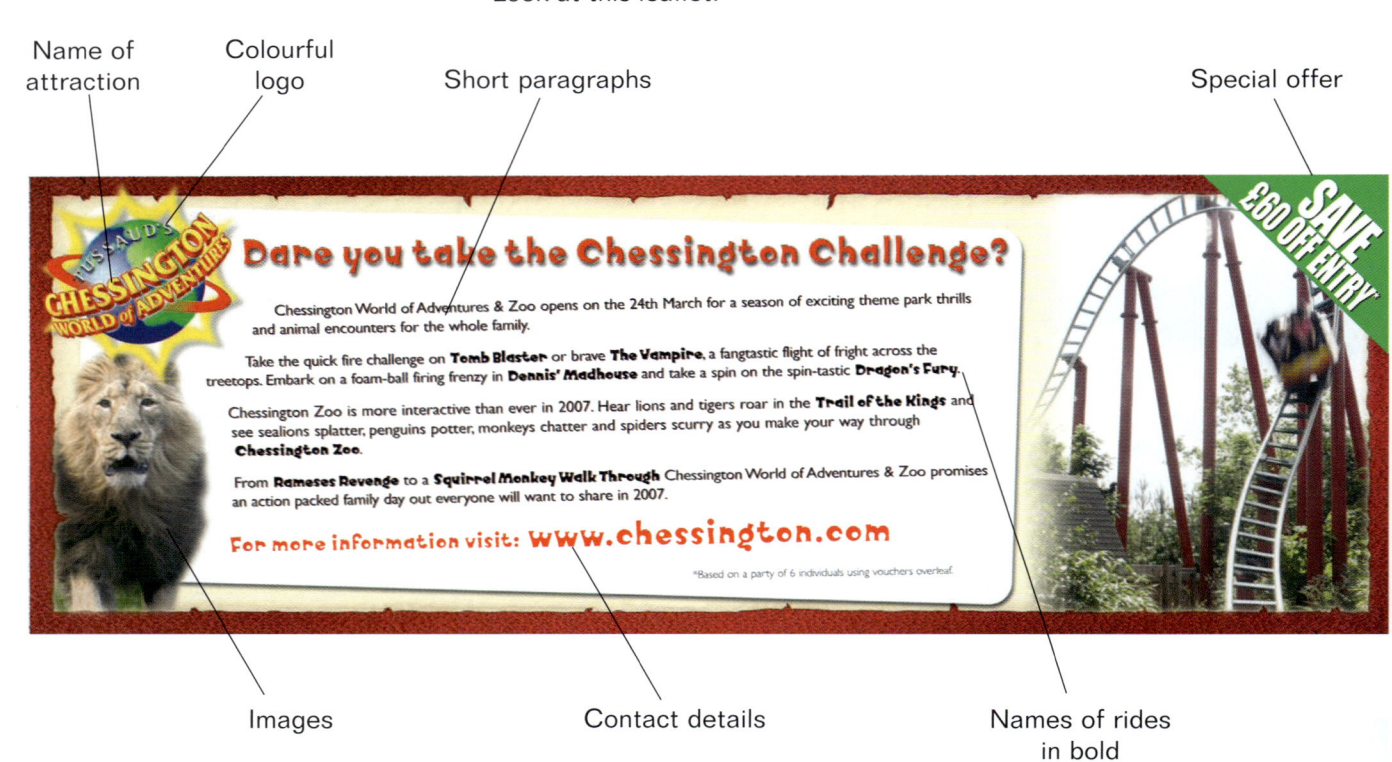

Labels: Name of attraction; Colourful logo; Short paragraphs; Special offer; Images; Contact details; Names of rides in bold

Dare you take the Chessington Challenge?

Chessington World of Adventures & Zoo opens on the 24th March for a season of exciting theme park thrills and animal encounters for the whole family.

Take the quick fire challenge on **Tomb Blaster** or brave **The Vampire**, a fangtastic flight of fright across the treetops. Embark on a foam-ball firing frenzy in **Dennis' Madhouse** and take a spin on the spin-tastic **Dragon's Fury**.

Chessington Zoo is more interactive than ever in 2007. Hear lions and tigers roar in the **Trail of the Kings** and see sealions splatter, penguins potter, monkeys chatter and spiders scurry as you make your way through **Chessington Zoo**.

From **Rameses Revenge** to a **Squirrel Monkey Walk Through** Chessington World of Adventures & Zoo promises an action packed family day out everyone will want to share in 2007.

For more information visit: **www.chessington.com**

*Based on a party of 6 individuals using vouchers overleaf.

SAVE £60 OFF ENTRY

2 Make a list of concrete nouns based on what you can see in the pictures on this leaflet. Then, next to each, write abstract nouns or ideas that these suggest to you. These are the associations the advertisers are hoping readers of the leaflet will make.

3 **a** What is the effect of the question in the title of the leaflet?
    b The advertisers use a number of devices such as imperative verbs, personal pronouns, alliteration, rhyme and 'made up' words. Find examples of these from the leaflet and explain their effect.

4 Using the Chessington World of Adventures leaflet as a model, you are going to design your own leaflet informing the public about a place of interest.

  a You will need to research this place and gather all the information you need before you start.
  b Decide who your target audience will be and brainstorm ideas about what would interest them and how you will appeal to them.
  c Make a list of points that you will include.
  d Decide how you will organise these points.
  e Design the layout of the leaflet, making sure that it is visually attractive. Do a mock-up of it using a piece of A4. You could fold the paper to divide it into different sections.

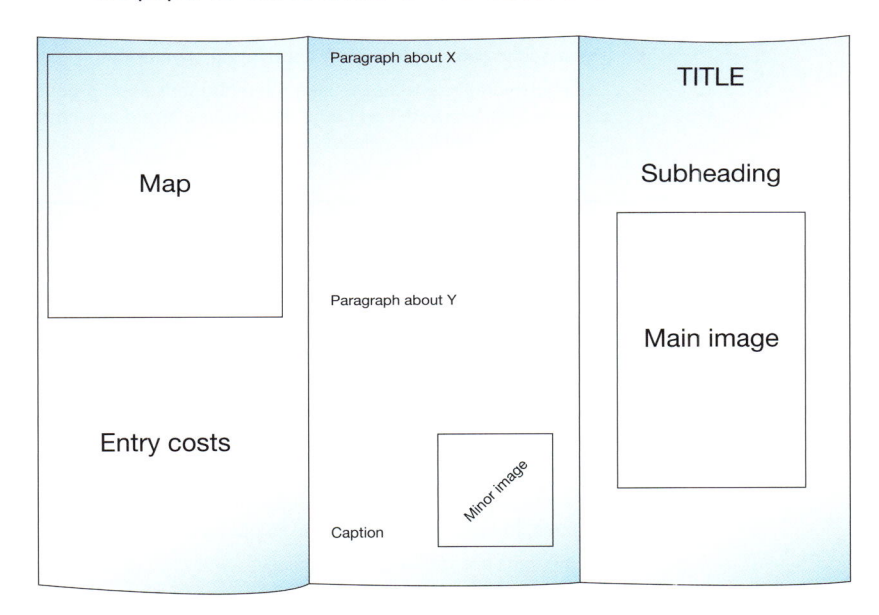

Taking it further

You are going to make your leaflet more interactive, so that your readers become involved in the product you are selling and informing them about.

- Think about how this could be done. Maybe you could include a quick quiz or some questions with hidden answers.
- Come up with a gimmick that will gain the readers' attention.
- Incorporate this into your leaflet.

[Leaflet layout diagram showing: Map, Entry costs | Paragraph about X, Paragraph about Y, Minor image, Caption | TITLE, Subheading, Main image]

  f Write the text for your leaflet, making sure that what you write is clear and that you use persuasive language (see Unit 22).
  g Use a word processing package to create the final piece.

How did I do?

I know that leaflets are produced by companies to inform, persuade or advise the public.	✔ ☐
I know that a leaflet must be presented and written clearly, and should be visually attractive.	☐
I know that persuasive language and gimmicks may be used to influence the readers.	☐

Teacher's tips

Remember, **concrete nouns** are names of things that can be experienced through your senses, so they can be touched/seen/heard/tasted/smelt. **Abstract nouns** are names of things that cannot be sensed, like ideas. A table is a concrete noun but happiness is an abstract noun.

115

Answers

Unit 1

1. We were just amusing ourselves, playing with a ball and drinking Coca-Cola, when a man came and said, 'Excuse me. What do you think you're doing?'
2. The man calls Pip a 'little devil' and easily turns him upside down.
3. The man is not particularly kind to children, is used to being obeyed, and may be violent.
4. The man's state suggests that he has been living rough out in the open, in unfamiliar surroundings. (He may even be more used to city life than the country.)
5. The coarse grey and the leg iron point to his being an escaped convict.
6. He eats 'ravenously' and apparently considers eating Pip.
7. He speaks non-Standard English. He is apparently not an educated man.

Unit 2

3. The sun is going down and night is about to fall, which makes the atmosphere all the more threatening. The sun being about to set also echoes Torak and Renn about to enter the cave.
4. Crimson is red and therefore suggests blood – of death or sacrifice.
5. The mountain is 'gaunt', has a 'flank' and is 'like the head of some giant creature'. All these suggest that it is alive, and may therefore be a threat.
6. The hole 'gapes' like the jaws of a monster and 'glares' like fierce eyes.
7. The 'seeping' mist sounds as if it is creeping up on Torak and Renn, and its 'tendrils reached for them' makes it sound like a carnivorous plant.
8. Calling it the Viper makes it sound dangerous.
9. It seems likely that Torak and Renn will enter the cave and meet extreme danger there!
10. The atmosphere is threatening. The factory being derelict makes it physically dangerous but also a possible hiding place for dangerous people.

Unit 3

1.
   a. Jack is relaxed, self-confident and active.
   b. She is proudly disdainful.
   c. She is furious.
   d. He appears to be relaxed and casual, but this may not be entirely genuine. His 'studying' passers-by suggests a purpose that is disguised by his relaxed pose.
   e. She is nervous and afraid.
2. This makes your eyes look cold and as if the smile is not genuine.
3. Hekken's eyes suggest he is unfeeling and uncaring, and may even enjoy making people suffer.
4. Hekken is violent and likes to take people by surprise.
5. He is dangerous in the same way as a snake.
6. He pretends to be reluctant to hurt his victim, and his polite, formal language shows that he enjoys pretending to be civilised.
7. He is playing with Sam, pretending to 'conspire' (share a secret plan) with him, as if they were equals rather than Hekken having all the power.
8. Hekken is far from straightforward. He loves cruelty and enjoys playing mind games with his victims.

9–10. These questions are open-ended, but Sam's account would reveal fear mixed with an underlying courage, and would probably express extreme dislike of Hekken. Hekken's would reveal the pleasure he takes in hurting and scaring people, and his contempt for Sam. We might be sure that he will break Sam before 'disposing' of him.

Unit 4

1.
   a. soft
   b. wizened
   c. swift
   d. ancient

   (Answers may vary.)
2. Her words are eerily hypnotic. Their effect is to lull Peer into a kind of trance. They are 'a low musical murmur like the stream in summer'.
3. Alliteration examples: *l*ove, *l*ook; *w*ater, *w*eary; *r*ank, *r*otten; *fl*owing, *s*o*f*t; be*st*, hi*ss*. They add to the hypnotic effect.
4. The mist makes the mood magical and mysterious, but the mood becomes suddenly more down to earth when it blows away.
5. Loki's barking wakes Peer from his trance by reminding him that he is needed.
6. 'All for the best, maybe.'
7. 'The rank, rotten, water smells' (smell); flowing in soft wreaths (sight and touch); 'a soft hiss', the barking (hearing).
8. The mood is eerie, hypnotically captivating, mysterious.
9. The short, jumpy sentences make the mood tense and urgent, showing that Macbeth and Lady Macbeth are afraid of what they have done, and of being discovered.

Unit 5

1.
   a. The enemy's arrows fell upon us like a deadly rain (suggests the movement of the arrows and the intentions of the enemy)
   b. The river twisted through the valley like either a giant snake or a silver ribbon (depending on whether you wanted the river to seem menacing or beautiful).
   c. I felt like a rat in a drainpipe ('a stick of rock in its wrapper' would be far too light-hearted for the situation!)

   (Answers may vary.)
2.
   a. She found her husband irritating or perhaps embarrassing at times, but had schooled herself to put up with it.
   b. She finds her father embarrassing.
   c. He is indicating danger.
3. This detail helps to create a relaxed, peaceful mood.
4.
   a. The alliteration suggests the flowing water.
   b. Less effective, because tautological?
   c. This is quite amusing as Boris is a dog; it suggests that he is uncontrollable.

5–8 Personal views and responses

Unit 6

1.
   a. over the field
   b. Except where the beetle flies making a steady, low buzzing sound
   c. that ivy-covered tower over there
   d. Disturb her in her long-accustomed, lonely watch
   e. The simple (or primitive) ancestors of the village lie buried.

2. The day's work is done and night draws in. This makes the poet relaxed but in the mood for thinking of things passing away.
3. The bell sounds to mark the end of the day.
4. The bell sounds, the cows and the plowman are going home, and it's getting dark.
5. the beetle and the sheep bells
6. people coming too close to her leafy hiding place
7. buried bodies
8. It makes it seem that nothing new is happening. The village and its churchyard have gone on in the same way for generations.
9. day – way, lea – me
10. As for question 8, the emphasis is all on things carrying on unchanged for centuries. The poem celebrates the way in which, though individuals die, the rural way of life continues.
11. This requires a personal response. However, the poem is largely about the passing of one generation after another, the humble virtue of even those who have never become famous, the passing of time, and – in the last few verses – about how the poet imagines he might be remembered after his own death. The form of the poem is quite traditional and the metre and rhyme scheme are very regular. The poet is not trying to surprise us with his style. This echoes the subject matter.
12. Shakespeare wrote mostly in blank (unrhymed) verse. Each line has five pairs of syllables, each pair consisting of one unstressed and one stressed. For example: 'There _is_ a _wil_low _grows_ a_slant_ a _brook_.' Gray's Elegy is the same as this.
13. Hopkins' poem is much more lively and energetic in form and language, expressing his excitement at seeing the bird, and the energy of the bird itself.

Unit 7

1. Some possible answers are:
   a. The father wants his son to be good at fishing, but the son is really more interested in books.
   b. The boy's father doesn't.
   c. They both want to be her boyfriend.
   d. She spends more time with her friends than she can afford if she also wants to practise. Her instructor says she has to choose.
   e. He steals one, and a boy who doesn't like him sees and threatens to report him.
2. There is tension between Miss Dunn and the girls, and between some of the girls.
3. Will the girls join in or not?
4. Will the girls disobey the authority of Miss Dunn?
5. Claire – she is rebellious.
6. She thinks they won't get away with it. She is more cautious and obedient to authority.
7. You might wonder if they do get away with it, or if something goes wrong. They might win by accident! The audience is interested in the dynamic between the girls and in the outcome of their 'skiving'.

Unit 8

1. Some other purposes: to inform, explain, describe, argue, persuade, analyse, review, advise, encourage
2.
   a. To entertain. The tone is casual ('several', 'Two or three') and uses descriptive detail to paint the scene. The idea of there being 'two or three' Draculas is amusing, as is the idea that they look at the writer 'pityingly'. The writer is encouraging us to laugh at his or her discomfort.
   b. To review/criticise. It gives a personal evaluation of the production ('partial success', 'convincingly wise', 'not always in tune').
   c. To advise. Using clear and simple language, it lists what the reader should and should not do.
   d. To inform. It gives clear information and options.
   e. To persuade. It uses adjectives that make Mallorca sound attractive, e.g. fashionable, historic, ancient, pretty.
3. To argue a case. It makes a statement – 'School uniform does little for pupil equality' – then gives two reasons to justify it. It uses 'Moreover', often used in formal arguments, and follows it with another logical argument. There is no attempt to persuade just by using appealing adjectives as in the paragraph on Mallorca.
5. Swift is pretending to be as uncaring about the suffering of the poor in Ireland as he thinks the British government must be to allow them to starve. It is his way of criticising the government.

Unit 9

1. _Teddy's Special Day_ – young children

   First Steps In Tropical Fish Care – people who want to know how to keep tropical fish

   The Great Philosophers: – serious-minded people who want to study philosophy

   Coping with Parents – teenagers who find their parents difficult

   Europe on a Dollar a Day – students or other young travellers with very little money

   Up Everest the Hard Way – either climbers or 'armchair adventurers' who want to enjoy the thrill of mountaineering by reading about someone else doing it

2.
   a. tourists /J. K. Rowling fans, possibly Americans: because of the information about Rowling and the word 'quaint'
   b. girls reading a magazine for teenage girls: a casual tone, girl-orientated slang
   c. young children: very simple
   d. relatively inexperienced cyclists: methodical and detailed instructions

3. The extract is from a specialist caving magazine. It includes a technical term – 'phreatic tube'; also phrases used in a special context by cavers – 'routine digging trip' (i.e. a caving trip on which cavers dig at the end of a passage in the hope of eventually breaking through into a new passage), and 'well-decorated chamber' (one with stalactites and stalagmites). The mention of the cave name, club name (CC means Caving Club) without any further explanation, plus the use of a nickname, suggest that this is aimed at a fairly small world, in which many club members are familiar with the things mentioned. The jokey informal phrase 'intrepid trio' reinforces this.

4. 'Neptune's ocean': educated audience who would know about myths; 'multitudinous seas incarnadine': educated – long Latin-based words; 'Making the green one red': a simple version for the less educated.

5. skateboarders; young women who own or like dogs; people interested in science (but not necessarily professional scientists)

Unit 10

2   a   'well-fed' horses: they could afford to feed them well, unlike the Native Americans

    'women and children butchered in the snow': makes the white man sound cowardly, heartless and cruel

    'herded': treated like animals

    'like twigs': weak and insubstantial

    b   'tuck into your turkey': you're well off

    'spare a thought': guilt – you have no real problems to worry about, and you may not care much about the poor and homeless

    'shivering . . . scavenging scraps': pity – she is cold and forced to live like an animal

    'if you don't care enough, don't let us spoil your Christmas': guilt if reader ignores the appeal

    c   'groans': guilt for making the planet suffer

    'poison': guilt

    'gas-guzzling cars': guilt

    'ripped out so that we can eat more hamburgers': guilt and sorrow

    d   'held hostage by young hoodlums': anger, indignation

    'prowl the streets . . . next victim': fear (it could be me . . .)

    'terrorise the elderly – who deserve peace and quiet': anger and pity for elderly people

    'thugs': anger

3   Paragraph 1 – it's beautiful and unspoilt; Paragraph 2 – it's about to be brutally ruined; Paragraph 3 – this is happening because of greed.

4   The passage makes us feel that something beautiful is going to be senselessly destroyed for the sake of a few people.

5   'home to a multitude of animals and birds'; 'tiny dormouse'; 'shy but brightly coloured woodpecker'; 'timid roe deer'; 'age-old paths'; 'symphony of birdsong'

6   'brutalised' – savaged by corporate greed (makes it seem like an act of bestial cruelty – as if greed is a monster); 'The sleeping dormouse will be rudely awoken by the ear-splitting sound of chainsaws' (makes it seem dreadful that the harmless little dormouse will be woken up so horribly).

7   They are 'fat and pampered', even too fat and lazy to walk around the golf course (they ride in buggies!).

8   The phrase 'add another few million to its overflowing bank account' makes it sound as if the company has too much money already.

Unit 11

1   Non-fiction: autobiographical account, description of a place someone has visited, newspaper article, police report, book review, journal, documentary

    Fiction: detective novel, Shakespearen play, poem

Unit 12

1   malevolent: wishing evil; brindled: grey with streaks; bard: poet; primeval: very old, relating to the origin of man; clan: tribe; blotched: spotted; leers: looks slyly

3   a   Rhythm varies between 7, 6 and 10 syllables per line but in total between 30 and 32 syllables per stanza; rhyme is ABCB.

    b   tail, hell, hard, crouches, laws, man, purr, demon's tail (Alternative words that make sense and rhyme and keep the syllable count will work but these are what the poet used.)

    c   Onomatopoeia: purr, silky, capers and claws; Alliteration: swings his snaky; bony, brindled; crouches and capers; curved sharp claws

    d   hate, snaky, hell, black, scorn, brute, demon

Unit 13

1   a   burly: strong and heavy; judicious: sensible; wizened: wrinkled; insipid: dull; coy: modest; eccentric: unconventional

    b   scowled: frowned, angry, unhappy; mumbled: spoke in a garbled way, unhappy, disgruntled; stormed: erupted, explosive, anger; glided: elegant, swift movement; sprang: jumped energetically, angrily; sauntered: strolled, power, time

    c   ferociously: fiercely, scary; languidly: lazily; heavily: lack of energy, tired, sad; passionately: energetically, keen; deprecatingly: ironically, critically

2   barrel-bodied; ham-like hands; scowling face; jauntily-tilted peaked cap; surged; waddled; ferociously; surveyed; turned; thems bastards; derogatory blast

3   'ham-like hands', makes Spiro sound chubby and meaty.

4   Direct speech and careful choice of vocabulary. The use of dialect aids Durrell's depiction.

5   The vocabulary is less precise in the rewritten version.

6   'pale and dwarfish': large, smooth-faced

    'an impression of deformity': well-made

    'murderous mixture of timidity and boldness': every mark of capacity and kindness

    'loathing and fear with which Mr Utterson regarded him': he cherished for Mr Utterson a sincere and warm affection

Unit 14

1   a   when characters and setting are introduced

    b   when some problem or conflict appears

    c   when the problem's consequences emerge and events unfold; the high point of the story, when events change

    d   when the movement towards an end occurs

    e   when problems are solved

2   internal: inside; external: outside

3   Sephy is confused about what to do and whether what she has done was the right thing. '. . . it was horrible. Everything was going wrong.'

4   Lola, Joanne and Dionee confront Sephy as she comes out of the toilet.

5   First person makes the event sound more real and immediate. We gain an insight into the narrator's thoughts.

Unit 15

1   a   traffic lights etc.: street; music etc.: night club/disco; desks etc.: office; check-in desk etc.: airport; candyfloss etc.: circus/fair

2   a   touch: slap, tickle, wince, sunburn, moist; sight: fanfare, pink, sunburn; hearing: tune, fanfare, whinny, silent hullabaloo, squealed, wheezed; taste: devoured, nibbled

    b   alliteration: ice-cream cornet, slap of sea, a wince and whinny; onomatopoeia: tickle of sand, slap of sea, bashing sea

    c   metaphors: slap of sea, tickle of sand, fanfare of sunshades opening, compromise of paddlers, a boy and a lion; similes: wild as seedcake, nibbled like a mouse

    d   tore, devoured, nibbled, hiccupped, capered, squealed, wheezed, dodged, warned, spread, hopped

Unit 16

1. a biased
   b unbiased
2. Biased words: yob, typical hooligan, hostile, rude
   Unbiased words: seemed, was
3. Tabloid: short paragraphs, colour pictures, stories about celebrities and football stars
   Broadsheet: lots of detail, few pictures, long articles
4. The Minister for Education has introduced a new ruling that secondary school children should have more homework. The shadow Education Minister disagrees with the new law and thinks children need more fresh air. Psychologists suggest that children have become depressed because of school pressures.
5. Fact: 'The Minister for Education spoke yesterday about his new bill to increase the amount of time secondary-aged children spend on homework.'
6. Opinion: 'nothing short of ludicrous'
7. to persuade readers that the new bill is a stupid idea
8. He selects one quotation from the opposing side which is very strongly expressed and does not counter it in any way. In fact, he provides support for this side by way of the psychologists' views.
9. a exaggerated
   b understated

Unit 17

1. a and c sound as if they are from a report; b does not.
2. He is poor, doesn't sleep much and is malnourished. His home is chaotic and noisy.
3. 'eyes as wide as a football-pool': he has bags under his eyes from a lack of sleep; 'ears like bombs': shape, or he hears a lot at home so his ears have exploded; 'teeth like splinters': badly taken care of; 'hair is an exclamation-mark': it is shocking and messy
4. His teeth are rotting, his hair is a mess, he is pale (his belly is white), his neck is dark and uncleaned, he has holes in his clothes, he is distracted in class, he sleeps in a sack in the kitchen at home rather than in a bed, his father and grandmother drink alcohol to excess, his mother ran off with another man, and he's given an aspirin to keep him quiet.
5. This suggests it is long and complicated to manoeuvre around.
6. The poem is like a prayer for Timothy Winters' life to change.

Unit 18

1. considerable, One may, companions, excessive, within the means, an extremely amusing diversion
2. Many people really enjoy going to the circus. You can go on your own or with friends. It's usually quite cheap and most families can afford it. It can be a great night out.
3a.
   - perhaps for a tourist guide or to claim protection for a particular church as being unique
   - What period is covered by 'medieval'? What were the main styles? What technical advances were there? Who were the famous architects? What were the differences in style?
   - internet, library
   - Architecture and History

   b.
   - for an art book or a biography
   - When did he live? Where did he live? What is so good about his art? What kind of man was he?
   - internet, library
   - Art history

   c.
   - for a local guide, or a talk to the local history society
   - What industries or types of farming have there been? Was anyone famous born here? Did anyone famous come here? What buildings were here? What were the local customs?
   - local library, possibly internet, local church or other old monument, old people, old maps
   - local history

   d.
   - to prepare for a holiday, or to write a book about ancient death rituals
   - How was mummification done? Why was it done? When was it done? What beliefs are associated with it?
   - library, internet
   - Egyptology

   e.
   - to become a zoo keeper, to research animal intelligence
   - Where do they live? What do they eat? What different types are there? Are they an endangered species? How intelligent are they?
   - library, zoo, aquarium, internet
   - Zoology

4.

Passage 1	Passage 2
1. Son of a glovemaker	1. Son of a farm worker
2. Grammar School, where he learned Latin, logic and history	2. Classical university education, learning Greek and geography
3. We do not know exactly when and why he moved to London, but by 1592 he was known as a playwright.	3. Perhaps moved to London to escape a poaching charge. By 1590 was writing plays. (Not quite a contradiction, but nearly)
4. Supported by Earl of Salisbury	4. Supported by Earl of Southampton
5. Wife Anne was much younger	5. Anne was older
6. They had three children: two daughters and a son, Hamnet	6. Four children, including son Hamlet (plague and Black Death same)
7. Career interrupted by an outbreak of smallpox	7. Career interrupted by plague
8. Plays performed for Elizabeth I	8. Plays performed for James I (also true!)
9. Died 1513	9. Died 1514
10. Wrote 154 plays and 38 sonnets	10. Wrote 38 plays and 154 sonnets

Unit 19

1 This is not a definitive list, but the matches below make sense.

Symbolic object	Theme
sword	hate (though Buddhists see it as a symbol of truth)
wall	divided communities
unicorn	magic
pen	truth (or knowledge)
fist	resistance to oppression
mountains	knowledge (or the mystery of universe)
whale	the mystery of the universe

2 Mr Pedanski's attitude towards Zero is very negative, and is especially unworthy of someone who is supposed to be helping the boys to become useful members of society. His low expectations of Zero do not help Zero to achieve anything.

3 Stanley believes in Zero's ability to learn.

4 education, literacy, the power of authority

5 He is saying that people may be more intelligent and able to learn than they appear to be, and that they should be encouraged to learn.

6 Gradgrind gives her no chance to show what she knows. He is dismissive towards her.

7 the purpose of education

8 education

9 Sachar explores personal potential; Dickens does this to some extent but is more interested in what education is for – the mechanical categorisation of mostly useless facts, or something else.

Unit 20

1 a The education was very poor.
   b A shop doorway is not much of a home.
   c It was not really a surprise.

2 a fact
   b opinion
   c fact
   d fact
   e opinion
   f fact (they *did* think it)

3 a Gorillas like to eat large quantities of fruit.
   b Elephants can spray themselves using their trunks.
   c Mickey Mouse is a lovable cartoon character.
   d It is against the law to impersonate a police officer.
   e Abraham Lincoln was President of the United States.
   f Professional footballers have excellent ball control.

4 The first article claims that the Prime Minister is almost lying; it also interprets figures as showing that street crime is out of control. It regards 2,305 unsolved muggings as a high figure and suggests (without offering any evidence) that it would be even higher if people were not too afraid to go out, and didn't have so little faith in the police that they do not bother to report crime. It does not mention the total number of muggings. This article does not support the Prime Minister. The phrases 'explain away' and 'massively' suggest bias.

The second article claims that the Prime Minister 'has welcomed' these figures and that they actually reflect an increase in the public reporting of crime, which in turn is the result of increased confidence in the police. It thinks that 2,305 is a low figure, compared with the total of 4,000. This article supports the Prime Minister. The phrases 'welcomed' and 'increased public confidence' suggest bias.

Unit 21

1 a Friendly and informal; uses slang and careless exaggeration.
   b Formal; uses words that come from Latin, such as 'inform' rather than 'tell', and 'require' rather than 'need'. It is also slightly long-winded.
   c Ironic and understated; it is clear that the author does not respect the President although he says that he does.
   d Romantic; uses words such as 'enfolded', 'trembling', 'manly' and 'sighed'.

2 The tone is understated and reasonable: 'full agreement', 'necessary explanations'.

3 'Many of us actually dislike milk and apples.'

4 'Milk and apples (this has been proved by Science, comrades) contain substances absolutely necessary to the well-being of a pig.' Of course he does not say what those 'substances' are!

5 the fear that Jones the farmer will return

6 Orwell describes him childishly 'skipping from side to side and whisking his tail'.

7 Most critics think it works well.

8 The pigs and humans have become identical – symbolising the way in which, in Orwell's eyes, the leaders who emerged from the Russian Revolution of 1917, like Stalin, became just as corrupt, self-seeking and greedy as the leaders of the previous regime, and the leaders of other capitalist (non-Communist) countries.

Unit 22

1 a I tried to cast my tackle into the centre of the stream. I might find a fish there.
   b She was beautiful. More important, she was brave. Both of these are desirable features in a trapeze artist.
   c I entered the room with an attempt at dignity. However, I trod on a toy train. The train had been abandoned by Ben. I skidded across the floor. I then landed in a heap. I looked like a clown.

2 It says the island is 'a mystery'.

3 They are relaxed. They are chatting casually. Whitney makes a joke.

4 He does this so that there will be a contrast when things start to go wrong. It also suggests that things can go wrong even when we are feeling secure.

5 They are in the tropics, passing an island. They are both hunters. Rainsford has good eyesight and is an excellent shot with a rifle.

6 The mood becomes more urgent. There is fast-moving action.

7 The reference to blood ('blood-warm waters') suggests that something life-threatening may occur.

8 Only one animal can reason. Read the story!

9 This is uncertain at this point, but it seems likely that he will encounter danger.

Unit 23

1. The first uses short, plain sentences; the second uses longer sentences, metaphors and more vivid verbs ('crept', 'hanging', 'flickering').
2. It makes us wonder what sort of strange creature is pursuing her.
3. The verbs tend to suggest brisk activity; e.g. 'leap', 'raked', 'scrambled'. The word 'raked' is quite unusual.
4. Susan's
5. 'A spear *sighed* over her shoulder.' This makes us hear the sound of the spear in the air very close to Susan. The word 'sighed' is a surprising choice as it makes the spear sound almost harmless.
6. The description of the creature is interesting, and emphasises that the scene is seen from Susan's viewpoint. The phrase 'pecking strides' suggests a brittle way of walking; saying 'the feet were taloned' is somehow more sinister than 'He had taloned feet'.
7. The verbs in Extract **b** are also active, though more dramatic than mysterious – e.g. 'leapt' and 'swooped'. The narrative viewpoint is partly objective – just the author telling the story (as with the details about the snowmobiles, which Alex couldn't really know in these circumstances). Garner makes the pursuit seem urgent by revealing the strangeness of the creature and the closeness of the spear. Horowitz emphasises the technology and the straightforward physical danger, without any sense of mystery. Horowitz uses one quite vivid metaphor: 'black flies swimming into his field of vision' to describe the men on snowmobiles.

Unit 24

1. zoology, etymology, entomology, psychology, biology, toxicology, radiology
2. arachnophobia (spiders), agoraphobia (open spaces), demophobia (crowds). See also: http://phobialist.com.
3.
   - poor people: little sympathy for the poor (**b** and **c**)
   - children: should be quiet and tidy, may be hit (**b** and **c**)
   - schoolgirls: should be humble, quiet and tidy (**c**)
   - religion: only Christians are civilised (**a** and **c**); it is the duty of Christians to educate others in 'Christian' virtues, such as humility, even if it makes them suffer (**c**)
   - exploration: it is exciting and there is much to discover (**a**)
   - foreigners: many are 'wild, bloodthirsty savages' (**a**)
4.
   a. It shows that Jews were hated and persecuted.
   b. Shakespeare's attitude seems more sympathetic in that this is a powerful speech which creates sympathy for the character, but he did not go out of his way to portray Shylock as a good man.

Unit 25

1. The use of the present tense makes the moment seem more important and almost dreamlike. The use of the future tense at the end creates a feeling of anticipation – wanting the question answered.
2.
   a. adventure (could also be crime)
   b. science fiction
   c. horror
   d. crime
3.
   a. the dangerous action, but also the active words such as 'hurled' and dramatic phrases like 'twisted in a mask of fury'
   b. the emphasis on aliens, planets and futuristic technology
   c. the moon, the graveyard setting, the false sense of security – we assume that there is something horrible and unnatural about the child
   d. the tough, worldly character of the officer in charge, the crime scene details, the expectation of some peculiar clue at the end
4. This is comedy sci-fi (like *The Hitchhiker's Guide to the Galaxy*).

Unit 26

1. Stresses are as follows.
   a. <u>By</u> the <u>shi</u>ning <u>Big</u>-Sea-<u>Wa</u>ter (four pairs of stressed and unstressed)
   b. O <u>what</u> can <u>ail</u> thee, <u>knight</u>-at-<u>arms</u> (four pairs of unstressed and stressed)
   c. Like the <u>leaves</u> of the <u>for</u>est when <u>Sum</u>mer is <u>green</u> (four triplets of two unstressed and one stressed)
2. It sounds like Native American drums.
3. Byron's poem does. It fits the Assyrians attacking on horseback.
4. Keats's poem. The fourth line makes it seem as if something is wrong or is fading away – like the sick knight.
5. only the second and fourth lines of each verse
6. It rhymes in couplets: AA BB, etc. This helps to create the effect of a strong, unstoppable force driving down on Sennacherib.
7. A haiku has three lines, consisting of five, seven and five syllables.

Unit 27

1. sly, dirty, slimy, vermin, disease, beady eyes, whiskers
2. He feels sorry for him and knows what it is like to hitchhike.
3. He is kind and empathetic.

4, and 5

Quotation from the text	What this shows
'Going to London, guv'nor?'	man is probably a Cockney
'ratty-faced man with grey teeth'	sly, doesn't take care of teeth
'eyes were dark and quick'	sly but clever
'He didn't seem to like that question'	had something to hide
'he was wearing a greyish-coloured jacket with enormous pockets'	hints at his 'profession'

6. Introduction: **b**
   Main body: **a**
   Conclusion: **c**

Unit 28

1. Hansel and Gretel; Goldilocks; Red Riding Hood; Cinderella; Snow White; Rapunzel
3. First extract – original; second extract – parody
4. The parody has modern references like 'OK! magazine', and 'football star'.
5.
   - Cinderella's stepfamily has been invited to the ball.
   - They will not let Cinderella attend.
   - Her fairy godmother arrives.
   - She uses her magic to create a carriage and dress for Cinderella and tells her to go to the ball but she must be back by midnight.
   - Cinderella goes to the ball and meets Prince Charming, but as the clock strikes midnight she rushes out leaving her shoe behind.
   - The prince is in love with Cinderella so he keeps her shoe as a clue to her identity.
   - He sends a messenger to all the houses with the shoe.
   - When the messenger arrives at Cinderella's house, her stepsisters rush around trying to fit their feet into her shoe.
   - Cinderella is able to fit her foot into the shoe and she and Prince Charming marry and live happily ever after.
6. exaggeration, understatement, ridiculous situations, word play, stating the obvious, detail
7. It is modernised and makes use of exaggeration.
8. The names of the characters are stereotypes; it draws on stereotypes of modern times – frivolous and shallow women; the word 'trap' is humorous; the contrast between 'tall, dark and handsome' and 'stupid' creates humour.

Unit 29

1. **b** and **c**
2. The servant-girl takes after her misuses.
   It was nigh on twenty minutes past two.
3. A strange shivering that ran from head to foot and a sinking pain in his heart.
4. 'In one moment he passed from a state of sleep to a state of wakefulness'; 'stricken speechless with terror'; 'he drew himself away to the left side'
5. He saw a woman who angled a knife towards him, into the mattress, as if trying to kill him.
7. The second – it's written in the first person using 'me', 'my' and 'I'.
8. The second – the language is more in keeping with an older text.

Unit 30

1. 'retrieve' is to get back; 'scrutinise' is to look closely or examine; 'amble' is to walk slowly; 'depressed' suggests a stronger sadness than the word 'sad'; 'crimson' is a shade of red; 'coarse' is rough, 'hard' is solid; 'agile' is nimble and able to move easily; 'sporty' indicates a fondness for sport; 'fragrant' suggests a nice smell
2. The sun appears for the first time in 40 years.
   May sees it for the first time and her grandmother dies.
3. May and her grandmother
4. 'mushroom cloud' – shape and texture; 'blistered' – sounds painful, indicates heat also; 'vacant' – empty of what? Leads us to think of many things.
5. Literally the darkness has ended but also metaphorically the sadness, or lack of hope, has ended.
6.
   a exaggerate
   b verbose
   c transparent
   d clarify
   e highlight
   f trip

Unit 31

1. Facts: **a**, **c**, **d**
   Opinions: **b**, **e**, **f**
2. Factual: 'After two weeks in Holland . . . father's'; 'We attended an American school'; The largest room served as living room . . . Alps'
   Exaggerated/to entertain: 'where students thought it a fun prank to aim lit Bunsen burners at one another'; 'guided purely by the twists and turns of European highways'; 'extravagant cost of six hundred dollars'
4. The first sentence uses more detail and a metaphor – 'maps of fate'; it also mentions Lake Geneva which we imagine is beautiful.
5. fun prank played by students; cuckoo clock and feather-tick beds; mullioned windows; mandatory ski outings
7. To help you: events – what happens; setting – place and time; conversations – with her mum; thoughts – narrator's views
8. Verbs: 'landed', 'wound up' – sound unplanned; 'lined' – gives a visual impression; 'chained' – humorous. adjectives: 'lit' Bunsen burners – suggests danger; 'fully furnished' chalet – a home from home

Unit 32

1. Manual: step-by-step instructions, clear language, technical jargon
   Article: clear language, details, history, facts and figures, reasons
2. He explains the two different taps he will discuss.
3. One is about washer taps, the other about ceramic disc taps.
4. He gives brief information about each kind of tap.
5. 'Turning the handle . . . shutting off the supply'; 'With reverse . . . the water off.'
   'They usually go from . . . people'; 'if there is a problem you have to replace a disc cartridge'.
7. What? No grass?; A giant desert; New life
8. Common nouns: dinosaurs, world, mammals
   Proper nouns: Earth, Triassic, Pangaea
   Abstract nouns: time, period, extinction etc.
9. Pangaea, Triassic
10. For example: Dinosaurs first appeared about 230 million years ago.
11. Audience: children interested in history and biology. The material is broken down into small and easily digested chunks. It is quite easy to understand, with some words explained.

Unit 33

1. **a** ludicrous, **b** nightmare, **c** joke, **d** inhumane
2. **a** Some people disagree with having to pay for a television licence.
   b The M25 gets congested and some people dislike travelling on it.
   c Public transport in the UK is criticised by some people for being unreliable.
   d Some people think capital punishment is not a justifiable punishment.
3. They make tasks easier; efficiency; speed; multiple calculations are possible; word-processing; desk-top publishing and other software; fewer queues in some situations
4. They replace humans; people lose jobs; they can break down; they can develop viruses; difficult to fix if you don't know how; expensive to buy
5. easy to do long calculations; machines develop faults; people lose jobs
6. 'However'; 'Another point'; 'On the plus side'
7. refers to 'you', making it personal to reader; refers to specific software; gives examples
8. Raising opponents' views: Some people believe; Others think that

   Suggesting a contrast: However; On the other hand; Whilst; Whereas

   Suggesting a comparison, similarity: Similarly; Likewise
9. For: gets students into work frame of mind; prepares students for later life; students look smart – representing school; gives students a sense of identity; makes it easier to identify a student on a trip; no issues with competing over clothes and style – bullying is avoided

   Against: can be expensive; students are all the same – lack of individuality; students are not relaxed – so not working well; too rigid; many countries and some schools in the UK don't require uniform; can be uncomfortable; can cause external bullying with rival schools

Unit 34

1. **a** Jane Austen was a nineteenth-century author who wrote *Emma*.
   b Cats are irritated by fleas, and benefit from occasional applications of flea powder.
   c Stephen Hawking, author of the influential work *A Brief History of Time*, is a leading figure in modern physics.
2. **St Cuthbert's School report, autumn term 1971**
   As a boy, Ronald was imaginative, determined, good at maths, but a loner.

   The *Shorehampton Echo*, 5 June 1983
   Shorehampton branch of Floyd's Bank target of £500,000 raid. Thin thief dug into the bank from across road. 'Mole' suspected. Welsh accent.

   The Man they called the Mole: A life of Ronnie Morgan
   Born Cardiff 1960, poor family. Quiet boy. Scholarship to private school. Only child, coddled by his mother. Father cold.

   BBC News report, 14 July 2006
   Ronald Morgan killed by bus in Piccadilly attempting to escape Bungay's Bank.

   ***Daily Sportsman*, 14 July 2006**
   Miscalculation led to death on 21st bank job.

   ***Trisha* magazine**
   Champagne lifestyle, 19 bank robberies (but see *Daily Sportsman*: 20). Sensitive, generous, animal-lover.

   Letter, 10 July 2006
   Loved mother, wanted to impress father. Intended to retire after Bungay robbery.
3. Ronald Morgan was an only child born into a poor family in Cardiff in 1960. Although a poor mixer, Ronald Morgan showed promise at school. He had a close relationship with his mother but his father's lack of warmth may have helped turn him to crime. His first recorded crime, in 1983, was a robbery at Floyd's Bank, Shorehampton, which netted £500,000. He went on to rob at least another 19 banks, usually by burrowing into them from underground. Described by a girlfriend as sensitive and generous, he lived well on the proceeds of his crimes until a miscalculation led to his death in 2006. Evidence suggests that at the time of his death he had decided to retire.

Unit 35

1. **a.i** means that education leads to success; **a.ii** means that it is worthwhile in itself.

   b.i is more extreme than **b.ii**, which does not rule out the possibility of money being important.

   c.i is more extreme than **c.ii**. Animals may have rights – but fewer of them than people.

   d.i is a moral judgement; **d.ii** relates to health.

   e.i says that people who were once criticised as terrorists may eventually be praised for resisting oppression; **e.ii** is more general and avoids judging terrorism.
2. **a** Young people have a tough time at school, partly because schools are large and individuals are overlooked. Pupils are under pressure both to do well and not to do well. The modern world with which young people are confronted is challenging and confusing.
   b Young people have an easy time these days. Schools are not perfect, but in some ways this is good for pupils. All pupils are capable of success but some are led astray. Single-sex schools may be one solution. The world does have problems, but it is up to young people to pull themselves together and solve them.
3.

Agree	Disagree
Schools are not perfect.	Young people have a hard/tough time.
Some pupils choose popularity over academic success.	All pupils are capable of success.
The world is a challenging place.	It is the responsibility of young people to solve the world's problems.

4. The first letter is more sympathetic. The second is more casual in tone (e.g. 'kids' instead of 'young people').

Unit 36

2. Tennyson's poem suggests that soldiers should be prepared to go to their deaths obeying orders unquestioningly: 'Theirs not to make reply, / Theirs not to reason why, / Theirs but to do and die'.
3. The world should regard them as glorious, romantic and noble ('glory', 'wild', 'wondered', 'noble').
4. Owen sees war as cruel, disgusting and the cause of terrible and pointless suffering – not at all glorious or noble, as Tennyson saw it.
5. The words 'fumbling', 'stumbling', 'flound'ring' suggest an ordinary human being, not a hero; the words 'froth-corrupted lungs, / Obscene as cancer, bitter as the cud / Of vile, incurable sores' make war sound disgusting.
6. Owen thinks that the idea of war being 'glorious' is a lie.
8. For some people, at least, war in the trenches (1914–18) made war seem wasteful of human life, futile and barbaric, whereas for many in Tennyson's time it still seemed glorious. (This is partly because relatively few soldiers took part in war in Tennyson's time, whereas many more men, including those who were not professional soldiers, fought in the First World War.)

Unit 37

2. He feels grief for the plight of his people.
3. He feels that white men are unsympathetic and untrustworthy; they make empty promises.
4. It emphasises the way in which white men have repeatedly talked and said 'good words' without any actual good coming of it. The repetition of 'good words' also contains an irony which expresses Chief Joseph's bitterness: if the 'good words' are just empty promises, they are not really good at all.
5. grief, anger, bitterness, contempt
6. This is a matter of opinion, but there is something very dignified and therefore effective in the relative simplicity of the speech and its repetition of key words.
7. This is powerful because most people feel that human beings should be treated at least as well as animals, if not better. The comparison shows how bitter Orlando is.
8. He is unhappy that his 'gentility' (noble character) is undermined by his lack of education.
9. angry rebelliousness
10.
    a. Chief Joseph is responsible for his entire tribe, whereas Orlando has only himself to worry about. Chief Joseph feels that his people have been treated unjustly; they have had their land taken away and many have died. Orlando feels that he has been treated unjustly; he has also had his rights taken away.
    b. There is some similarity in the emotions, in that they both feel the victims of a great injustice done by someone more powerful. However, Chief Joseph has more sadness and is more resigned to the situation, whereas Orlando is more resentful and is beginning to feel an urge to rebel.
    c. Chief Joseph is more measured and dignified in his expression; Orlando uses a certain amount of emotive exaggeration when he compares himself with his brother's animals.
11. Answers should include the idea that Shylock is bitter about being the victim of racial prejudice, and is therefore insisting that he is human. He threatens revenge, whereas Orlando just wants his rights. Caliban is bitter about losing his island to the newcomers, and about being enslaved by Prospero.
12. Both Chief Joseph and Mark Antony use the repeated phrases in a bitterly ironic way, meaning more than the words on their own seem to say.

Unit 38

1.
    a. Arabic
    b. Arabic – meaning hashish-eater
    c. Gujerati, from Hindustani
    d. Hindi from Sanskrit, for an image of Krishna carried in procession
    e. Norwegian
    f. Algonquian, a Native American language
2. Bathsheba cannot meet the soldier's gaze. She also seems to think of herself as helpless. She is reluctant to let him look at her or touch her hand, and she is very embarrassed when he compliments her on her looks. He addresses her as 'miss', but the way in which he compliments her would seem unsubtle and possibly sexist nowadays.
3. 'obliquely noticed'; 'vexed'; 'infuse into a position of captivity'
4. It means she spoke with as much dignity as she could manage, given her rather undignified situation. The phrase sounds old-fashioned to us because of the complicated idea of infusing (something like injecting) an abstract quality – dignity. In addition, dignity, as a virtue, is less highly valued now than it was in Hardy's day.
5. 'guy in a beat up leather jacket'; 'that was it'; 'I guess'; 'it was like – I can't explain'; 'y'know? I mean everything. Things I thought I knew. Stuff I'd been taught.'
6. Zoe is imagining how her parents see her – as a child. The view is ironic: it is not how she sees herself at all.
7. It is a paragraph on its own, yet grammatically it is not even a sentence.

Unit 39

1.
    a. The girls overtook the boys. In version 1 the boys sound weaker and the focus is on them. In version 2 the focus is on the girls.
    b. The dog has eaten your dinner. Version 1 emphasises the fate of the dinner; version 2 focuses on the dog – perhaps it is ill as a result.
    c. Someone gave me a helping hand. Version 1 emphasises the neediness of the speaker.
    d. 'We have made mistakes,' said a government spokesman. Version 1 avoids admitting blame.
    e. Older boys led him astray. Version 1 emphasises the innocence of the person led astray; version 2 focuses more on the wickedness of the older boys.
2. The 4th boy's opening line is menacing, but some of his fellow brown eyes are still nervous. When they insult the Loner they are 'still only half serious', but their seriousness gradually increases. The threat becomes gradually more physical, especially with the 4th boy trying to make the Loner tie his lace. There is great tension in this moment, as we wait to see if the Loner will obey.
3. It is engaging because the audience can see what is going on and the Loner cannot.
4. This is a matter of opinion, but many would say the Loner.
5. The 4th boy appears to have most power. The teacher has engineered the whole situation but is barely in control of it.
6. There is no correct answer here, but what actually happens in the play is that the other blue-eyed pupils surge forward and rescue the Loner.

7   It would be reasonable to expect the scene to become more chaotic and violent – which it does, as the two groups gradually come to believe in their differentness.

8   There is no correct answer here. One could say Mr Wright's methods seem effective in that he has persuaded the class to divide in a way which reflects the way in which prejudice often works. However, he lacks control over the outcome, and there is no guarantee that the pupils will eventually understand the point being made about prejudice.

Unit 40

1   **a**   The audience would be used to candlelight and watching plays onstage.

   b   International travel was by sea, and ships would be at the mercy of the weather. Wild boar were still hunted in the forests – which covered much more of the land than now.

   c   This also reflects the importance of sea travel in Shakespeare's time.

2   Juliet shows her respect to her father in her meek and obedient tone and in her kneeling to him to plead with him. Few teenage girls would behave in this way now.

3   Capulet's tone reflects the fact that he expects his daughter to obey him in everything – even to marry the man he chooses. His fingers itch because he can hardly prevent himself from hitting or strangling her.

4   His reference to God shows that people in Shakespeare's time were religious and saw children as being lent to them by God. Many would also believe literally in curses.

5   The passages show that people were superstitious and believed in portents – signs of what was going to happen. On the other hand, there was a general belief that what was decreed by God (or the gods, as Caesar says) could not be avoided. The great debate was whether people really had no control over their lives – their fate being 'in our stars', or whether they could be 'masters of their fates' and change their lives by their choices and actions.

Unit 41

1   **a**   an apparently happy situation which the person enjoying it does not realise cannot last

   b   It's disappeared without trace.

   c   It makes no sense.

   d   He will not compromise.

   e   Make the most of what is unavoidable.

   f   Don't insist on formality.

   g   no sense or meaning

   h   What on earth! (an exclamation of disbelief)

2   **a**   'Purple' – emphasising its unusualness

   b   'Purple' and 'perfumed' begin with the same sound; this sounds harmonious but it also links the two words as contributing to the same exotic effect.

   c   The image is of the winds being in love with the sails.

3   He says the water loves (is 'amorous of') the strokes of the sails. Note the double meaning of 'strokes'.

4   Shakespeare's image of the boys, 'like smiling Cupids', is more compact and immediate in its effect than North's explanation of Cupid as portrayed by painters.

5   Shakespeare's version is much more fanciful. It makes Cleopatra seem more exotic, and like a goddess of love.

6   Henry's speech is rousing rather than hypnotic. The rhythm is strong and the language lacks the fanciful imagery of the Cleopatra speech. The style fits a pre-battle address to an army.

7   The extra syllable slows the line down, making us pause to take in the full drama of 'Burn'd on the water'. In Henry's speech, the extra syllable emphasises the word 'brothers', since it is a very unusual thing for a king to call himself the brother of common soldiers.

Unit 42

1   **a**   history

   b   tragedy

   c   comedy

2   **a**   a tragedy (*Hamlet*). We know this because it includes violence, murders, treason, revenge – and no jokes (except a very grim pun on the word 'union', which means both a pearl and the joining of husband and wife – Claudius and Gertrude).

   b   a comedy (*Twelfth Night*). It features some relatively lowly characters (who therefore speak in prose), planning to trick another character just for fun. Their trick also promises confusion involving love. There is also some straightforward punning: 'And your horse now would make him an ass.'

3   These words have all become more general in meaning. People use 'tragedy' for things that are just quite unfortunate (e.g. a football team losing); 'comedy' is anything funny; 'romance' usually refers to people falling in love; 'history' has changed the least, but is still more general now.

Unit 43

1   The play is likely to be about love and romance.

2   This is a metaphor, meaning that music encourages feelings of love.

3   the breeze

4   This speech suggests that Orsino is in love, but is rather self-indulgent in his love. He seems to enjoy his longing. It also suggests that he is not very constant: he gets tired of the music very quickly.

5   The order is c, a, d, e, b.

8   Helena and Demetrius fall in love.

9   love and disorder/confusion

10 There is a great deal of confusion, with people being made to fall in love with the 'wrong' partners, before all this is finally sorted out and everyone is happy.

Unit 44

1   metaphor

2   the bad things that luck makes happen to you

3   killing himself

4   The question is, is it better to live or die? Is it better to put up with all the suffering that luck throws your way, or to defeat all those troubles by killing yourself?

5   She appeals to his pride and sense of himself as a 'manly' man.

6   She wants to make it seem that she would be 'brave' enough to commit even the worst violence if she had sworn to do so, and that if he is a real man he should be prepared to do at least as much as her.

7   She is emotionally manipulative. She knows her husband's weak points and exploits them to persuade him to do what she wants.

8   physical courage and fighting prowess

9   He is brave when it comes to physical threats but he is afraid of the supernatural. His fear also reflects his sense of guilt at having murdered Banquo. He is afraid that he will go to hell as a result.

10 She seems to be more ambitious than Macbeth and less worried about the morality of how she gets what she wants. She is also more manipulative – though it could be argued that in Shakespeare's time women had to be manipulative to have any power at all.

Unit 45

1

Shakespeare's word	Meaning
purpose	intend, plan
spotless, unspotted	guiltless, innocent
arbitrement	decision by contest (e.g. by a battle)
peradventure	perhaps
perjury	breaking a promise
bulwark	defence, safeguard
gored	bloodied, wounded

2   Henry says that a king's responsibility towards his people is limited – that he cannot be held responsible for his subjects' sins.

3   planned murder; using false promises to trick virgins into having sex with them; looting and stealing

4   his soldiers

5   himself (This is the 'royal we': kings and queens refer to themselves as 'we'.)

6   He calls it 'idle', so he thinks it is useless.

7   He seems to think that a king has a heavy burden of responsibility, and that the official respect he receives does not make up for this.

8   He is saying that kings have a lot to worry about and therefore cannot sleep.

Unit 46

1   a   good and evil, the power of love, hate, size doesn't matter
    b   good and evil, family life
    c   home, safety
    d   magic, poverty

2   religion, family life, bullying, abuse, friendship

3   'longs to have friends'; 'strict religious group'; 'Taunted and bullied'; 'secret'; 'trapped'

4   'And' – sounds monotonous, reflects the idea of restriction.

5   never, shut, not, graves, tombstones, black, binding, briars

6   He saw organised religion as restrictive and stunting.

7   'Chapel', 'Thou shalt not', 'priests'

8   He suggests that the innocence and freedom of youth is replaced by dark restrictive adulthood and religion is its agent.

9   'gowns' and 'rounds'; 'briars' and 'desires'

10 The rhyme traps the words in the same way that religion traps people.

Unit 47

1

Informal	More formal
get across	convey
show	portray
person in the story	character
says again	repeats
beat	rhythm
writes the opposite	contrasts

2   b – it sounds more formal and is more detailed.

3   The first introduction is very direct, which is good. It is focused on the question but offers only one point centred on the form of the poem rather than meaning, suggesting that the essay will only focus on the rhyme of the poems. The second introduction is better as it not only focuses on the question but indicates the concepts that will be discussed in the essay. A combination of the two would be ideal.

6   Main point – red, evidence – yellow, analysis – blue, development – green

    a   It is evident from the first sentence that the theme of marriage is an important part of the novel. Austen writes 'It is a truth universally acknowledged that a single man in possession of a good fortune must be in want of a wife'. Not only is the theme of marriage important, but the fact that money plays its part in marriage at this time is also clear. Mrs Bennet's insistence that her husband visit Mr Bingley to secure an invitation and hopefully a husband for one of her daughters proves that for women of the eighteen hundreds, marriage and money went hand in hand.

    b   Marriage is a key theme in the book. Austen opens her novel with a famous line: 'It is a truth universally acknowledged that a single man in possession of a good fortune must be in want of a wife' and this shows how important marriage is in the novel. Everyone knows it – it is 'universally acknowledged', as Austen says. How different characters see marriage is what I will now look at.

Unit 48

1   *Romeo and Juliet*, *Macbeth*, *Othello*, *King Lear*

2   Sophocles was a Greek playwright. The chorus was a group of actors in ancient Greek drama who sang or spoke together, commenting on the significance of events in the play – they were like narrators.

3   They narrate events and explain events and consequences.

4   *Antigone*: 'She's thinking she's going to die'

    A View from the Bridge: 'watched it run its bloody course.'

5   *Antigone*: 'But there's *nothing to be done* . . . she's *going to have to play* her part right through to the end.'

    A View from the Bridge: 'sat there as *powerless* as I and watched it run its bloody course.'

6   *Antigone*: 'Thinking. She's thinking . . .' 'rise up against everyone. Against Creon'; 'hurtling further and further'

    A View from the Bridge: 'And now we are . . . Now we . . .'

7 Metaphor: 'hurtling further and further away from her sister Ismene' – not literally hurtling; 'green scent of the sea' – the scent is not literally green.
Miller uses personification: 'swallowing the tonnage of the world' – personified, to sound as if New York is eating trade. The playwrights also use alliteration: 'sitting there silent. Staring . . .'; 'seaward side . . .' 'green scent of the sea'.

8 *Antigone*: 'she's going to die . . . preferred to live'
A View from the Bridge: 'quite civilised . . . no longer keep a pistol'

9 references to fate and to history

Unit 49

1 a devastation: complete destruction, sadness, chaos
   b carcasses: death, darkness, blood
   c bloodstained: red, spattered, deep, indelible, permanent
   d procession: long organised line
   e wrecks: chaos, devastation

2 'maze'

3 'the apartment houses of the French Concession rose like advertisement hoardings in the August sunlight' – simile suggests irony. The devastation does not fit the positive idea of an advert. 'Craters like circular swimming pools covered the paddy fields' – the large size of the holes is suggested and irony is used again as the pools were a symbol of the opulent ex-patriot lifestyle in China before the occupation but now they symbolise devastation, decay and emptiness (through the comparison to craters).

4 'brown surface broken', 'devastation', 'Craters. . . covered the paddy fields', 'carcasses', 'attacked', 'dismantled', 'scattered'

5 rose, lay, floated, scattered, torn

6 adjectives, e.g. 'bloodstained'

7 sad and haunting

8 This is the original: A humid morning sun filled the stadium, reflected in the pools of water that covered the athletic track, and in the chromium radiators of the American cars parked behind the goal posts at the northern end of the football pitch. Supporting himself against Mr Maxted's shoulder, Jim surveyed the hundreds of men and women lying on the warm grass. A few prisoners squatted on the ground, their sunburnt but pallid faces like blanched leather. They stared at the cars, suspicious of their bright grilles, with wary eyes.

Unit 50

1 a rated: berated, scorned
   b usance: interest charged on money lent
   c cur: dog
   d gaberdine: Jewish coat
   e rheum: spittle
   f ducat: coin
   g thine: your
   h thee: you

2 his charging of interest and his business practices

3 dog: 'cut-throat dog', 'cur', 'dog'

4 For example: 'Hath a dog money?', 'You, that did void your rheum upon my beard . . .'

5 'For sufferance is the badge of all our tribe.'

6 He suggests Shylock should lend the money as if to an enemy who may exact a penalty against him if he breaks the contract.

7 Irony, sarcasm, anger. He is indignant at being asked for a favour by the very person who has mistreated him in the past. The question mark at the end of this line suggests his indignation and sarcasm. He is not asking a genuine question, more a rhetorical one.

8 revenge

9 anger at being treated so badly, feeling momentary power and wishing to make the most of it, upset and bitter

Unit 51

1 First person: **a** and **c**
   Third person: **b** and **d**

2 third person

3 The narrator knows what Mr Bingley did and hoped to have done and what the ladies had seen.

4 Mr Bingley returned Mr Bennet's visit. The ladies saw him approach the house. He was wearing a blue coat and he arrived riding a black horse. He sat downstairs for ten minutes in the library with Mr Bennet, but they stayed upstairs.

5 First person: more personal, thoughts and feelings are conveyed more directly to reader. Disadvantages are that we are not distanced from the reader and cannot judge actions impartially. Some people mistakenly take first person narration for autobiographical accounts.
Third person creates more distance, which can sometimes be advantageous but can also make the writing less direct. We do not empathise as strongly with the narrator as a result.

6 intrigue, confusion, fear

Unit 52

1 Captain Gus Eckert, throttle, pod, deck, terrain, surface, Heat-Ray, nutrition

2 hooded, small, fast and armoured

3 'There was no screaming or shouting, but a silence'; 'Then a hoarse murmur and a movement of feet'; 'A woman thrust at me with her hand and rushed past me. I turned with the rush of the people'; ' "Get under water!" I shouted'.

4 'a movement of feet'; 'a splashing'; 'A woman thrust at me with her hand and rushed past me'; he is 'unheeded' 'when he shouts; 'The splashes of the people in the boats leaping into the river'; 'People were landing hastily on both sides of the river. . . . the people running this way and that. . .'

5 'The splashes of the people in the boats leaping into the river sounded like thunderclaps in my ears' – simile suggests panic and noise.
'But the Martian machine took no more notice for the moment of the people running this way and that than a man would of the confusion of ants in a nest against which his foot had kicked' – simile suggests insignificance and small size of humans compared with Martian machine.

6 Martians, Heat-Ray, creatures, machine, batteries, generator

Unit 53

3. thee, thou
4. He has personified death, made it more real.
5. Shakespearean. Rhyming couplet at the end
6. ten or eleven syllables following 'unstressed, stressed' pattern: de-<u>dum</u> de-<u>dum</u> de-<u>dum</u> de-<u>dum</u> de-<u>dum</u>
8. sleep
9. It suggests that death is not as powerful as it thinks it is.
10. 'Fate, chance, kings, and desperate men'
11. Death can be imitated by using poppy (opium) or charms (sleeping potions).
12. When we die we enter eternal life and therefore death is defeated.

Unit 54

2. 'trumpet summons' – calling them; 'twilight struggle' – struggle at its end
3. 'not . . . but . . .'; 'rejoicing in hope, patient in tribulation'
4. A list. This builds up a feeling in the audience of enmity against a series of forces amongst which people will recognise or have experienced at least one, which unites the audience with him in his purpose.
5. He referred to 'we' and asked questions.
6. rhetorical question – includes audience and gets them thinking
7. For example: 'year in and year out' – repetition; 'grand and global alliance' – alliteration; 'defending freedom' – elevates his struggle and uses metaphor; 'The energy, the faith, the devotion' – cluster of three; 'His blessing' – allusion to God and religion; 'glow from that fire' – extended metaphor

Unit 55

1.
   a. prospective students or parents
   b. someone wanting to visit an entertainment
   c. someone wishing to rent or buy a house
   d. a building company/government
   e. tourists
   f. tourists
   g. theatre-goers
2. lion – dare, bravery, challenge, king, the wild, nature
   ride – fun, exhilarating, dangerous, alive, life, speed, movement
3.
   a. It directly appeals to readers and challenges them to prove their bravery. It suggests Chessington World of Adventures is truly an adventure where your bravery will be tested.

   b. take, brave, embark and hear; Dare you, as you make your way; fangtastic flight of fright, sea-lions splatter, penguins potter; spin-tastic and fangtastic. The imperative verbs are direct and the pronouns make the leaflet seem personal and appealing to readers. The language devices make the words and leaflet more memorable.